SOUTHWEST ENGLAND BY ROAD

A COMPREHENSIVE GUIDE TO DEVON, SOMERSET, CORNWALL, AND EVERYTHING IN BETWEEN

Written by: Harrison Walshaw

1st Edition

Disclaimer

This guidebook, "Southwest England by Road" contains general information only. While every effort has been made to provide accurate, reliable, and up-to-date information, the authors and publishers make no representations or warranties, express or implied, as to the completeness, accuracy, or suitability of the information contained within. Any reliance placed on this information is strictly at your own risk.

Under no circumstances will the authors or publishers be liable for any loss, damage, or inconvenience arising from the use of this guide, including, but not limited to, indirect or consequential loss or damage. The inclusion of any links or recommendations does not necessarily imply an endorsement of the views expressed within them.

Travel information is subject to change, and, therefore, readers are advised to confirm essential travel details with relevant authorities or service providers before embarking on their journey. The authors and publishers are not responsible for any errors or omissions, or for any decisions made based on the information provided in this guide.

Please be aware that travel regulations, visa requirements, and other related information are prone to change. It is the responsibility of the reader to stay informed about current travel advisories and requirements.

We hope that this guidebook serves as a valuable resource and inspiration for your travels. Wishing you a safe and memorable journey as you discover the beauty and wonders of these remarkable regions!

Cover Image Credit © Nickos via Canva, https://www.canva.com/photos/MADyWyvou28/

Contents

INTRODUCTION

WELCOME TO THE JOURNEY

Welcome, fellow traveler, to a journey through the heart and soul of South West England. This guidebook, "Southwest England by Road: A Comprehensive Guide to Devon, Somerset, Cornwall, and Everything In Between," is your companion to discovering some of England's most breathtaking landscapes, rich history, and vibrant cultures.

As you flip through these pages, imagine embarking on a personal adventure that takes you through quaint villages, along rugged coastlines, and across peaceful countryside settings. This journey is more than just a trip; it's an exploration of diverse stories, local flavors, and unique traditions that make Devon, Somerset, and South West Cornwall so special.

Visualize the wild, open landscapes of Dartmoor's moors, where ponies wander freely and ancient stone circles stand as silent witnesses to history. Envision the serene beaches of Cornwall, where the rhythmic waves of the Atlantic create a soothing soundtrack and the sunsets paint the skies in brilliant hues.

Stroll through the historic lanes of Somerset, where each corner reveals a blend of Roman and medieval marvels, offering a journey through time. Experience the artistic heartbeat of places like St. Ives, where art galleries and studios showcase the creative spirit of Cornwall.

This guide will lead you through a spectrum of experiences – from the thrill of surfing on Cornwall's waves to the calm of a countryside stroll. You'll discover culinary delights in bustling market towns, where each dish tells a story of the land and its people.

Whether this is your first glimpse of the English countryside's allure or a return to these unspoiled terrains, the regions of Devon, Somerset, and South West Cornwall are brimming with discoveries waiting for you. Engage with the locals, whose stories and hospitality bring depth and warmth to your journey.

Let this book serve not just as a guide, but as a source of inspiration for adventure, a wellspring of daydreams, and a foundation for unforgettable memories. Each chapter, each recommendation, is your gateway to awe-inspiring moments, joy, and unexpected delights.

So, pack your curiosity, ignite your sense of adventure, and dive into the enchanting world of Devon, Somerset, and South West Cornwall. The road ahead is rich with discovery, where every turn brings a new story to life.

HOW TO USE THIS GUIDE

This guidebook is tailored to be both versatile and thorough, ensuring you have all the information you need, whether you're planning a detailed itinerary or embarking on an impromptu adventure.

Choose Your Adventure: We've organized this guide into distinct sections, each dedicated to one of the three regions: Devon, Somerset, and South West Cornwall. Feel free to jump straight to the part that most captures your imagination, or follow the guide in a way that aligns with your travel route.

Curated Itineraries for Every Traveler: Whether you have a weekend or several weeks, we've got you covered. Our carefully crafted itineraries cater to different durations and interests, ensuring you make the most of your time in these picturesque locales.

Tours Tailored to Your Interests: Are you a foodie, history buff, or traveling with family? Our special interest tours are designed to cater to your passions, providing targeted recommendations for a truly personalized experience.

Maps and Visual Inspirations: Use the detailed maps to navigate with confidence and soak in the beautiful photography that captures the essence of each destination. These visuals are not just guides but also a preview of the wonders awaiting you.

Practical Tips for Seamless Travels: In the final sections, you'll find essential information on accommodations, dining options, transportation, and more, designed to make your trip smooth and enjoyable.

Remember, this guide is your launchpad into the vibrant world of South West England. While it's here to offer direction and insight, the real magic of travel comes from the unexpected discoveries and spontaneous choices you make along the way.

A GLIMPSE INTO DEVON, SOMERSET, AND CORNWALL

Devon

Devon invites you to experience its dual coastlines - the rugged cliffs of the north contrasted with the serene sandy beaches of the south. Inland, the heart of Devon is a treasure trove of rolling hills, hidden valleys, and the wild expanses of Dartmoor and Exmoor. This is a place where ancient history and modern life blend seamlessly, offering everything from quaint villages to vibrant cities.

Somerset: Rustic

Somerset, a county of rolling countryside, is a patchwork of lush fields, apple orchards, and ancient woodlands. It is steeped in folklore and tradition, with historical gems like the Roman Baths in Bath and the mystical Glastonbury Tor. The region's rich agricultural heritage is celebrated through its famous cider and cheese, making it a haven for food enthusiasts.

Cornwall: Coastal Splendor and Artistic Heritage Cornwall is a symphony of spectacular coastal scenery, with its picturesque harbors, dramatic cliffs, and golden beaches. It is a land that has inspired artists for centuries, evident in its thriving arts and crafts community. From the surfers' paradise in Newquay to the artistic haven of St. Ives, Cornwall is a place of relaxation, creativity, and adventure.

PART 1: THE ESSENTIALS

PLANNING YOUR TRIP

Finding Your Path: Begin by identifying what you most want to see and do. Are you drawn to the rugged cliffs and surf beaches of Cornwall, the historical treasures of Somerset, or the natural beauty of Devon's national parks? Decide on your must-visit destinations and then map out a route that connects these highlights. Remember, flexibility can lead to the most memorable adventures.

Duration and Timing: Consider how much time you have. A weekend, a week, or longer? Each duration offers different possibilities and requires different planning strategies. Also, think about the timing of your trip. Some attractions may be seasonal or have varying hours throughout the year.

Accommodations and Reservations: From cozy bed-and-breakfasts to luxurious hotels, the region offers a wide range of lodging options. Book in advance, especially during peak seasons, to secure your ideal accommodations. Consider staying in various types of places to experience the diverse hospitality of the region.

TRAVEL TIPS AND ETIQUETTE

Respect Local Customs: South West England is rich in history and tradition. Respect local customs and traditions, especially in smaller villages and rural areas. A friendly attitude and a willingness to engage with locals can enrich your travel experience.

Sustainable Travel: Be mindful of your environmental impact. Consider eco-friendly travel options where available and respect natural sites, especially in protected areas like national parks.

Safety First: Always prioritize safety, especially when engaging in outdoor activities or exploring remote areas. Familiarize yourself with local emergency services and keep a basic first aid kit handy.

SEASONS AND WEATHER

Each season in Devon, Somerset, and Cornwall paints the landscape with a unique palette and brings its own set of experiences.

Summer (June - August): This is when the region shines brightest, with long, sunny days making it perfect for beach-going, hiking, and outdoor festivals. Coastal towns buzz with activity, and the sea offers a refreshing respite. However, this is also peak tourist season, so expect larger crowds and higher prices.

Spring (March - May): A time of renewal, spring sees gardens and woodlands come alive with colorful blooms. The weather is milder, making it ideal for exploring the countryside. It's also a quieter season, offering a more relaxed experience.

Autumn (September - November): Autumn cloaks the landscape in warm hues. It's a wonderful time for long walks, as the weather is still pleasant, and the summer crowds have dispersed. The harvest season also brings a variety of food and drink festivals.

Winter (December - February): Although colder and wetter, winter has a unique charm. Coastal storms can be dramatic, and the crisp air is invigorating. It's a great time for cozy pub visits and exploring indoor attractions like museums and galleries. Note that some outdoor attractions and accommodations may be closed or have limited hours.

Preparing for the Weather

Layer Up: The key to comfort in this region is layering. The weather can change quickly, so wearing layers that you can add or remove as needed is wise.

Rain Gear: Always pack a waterproof jacket or umbrella. Rain can come unexpectedly, regardless of the season.

Footwear: Comfortable, sturdy footwear is essential. Whether you're navigating cobblestone streets in historic towns, hiking in national parks, or strolling along the beach, the right shoes will make all the difference.

Sun Protection: Don't underestimate the sun, especially near the coast and during summer. Sunscreen, hats, and sunglasses are must-haves.

Winter Essentials: If you're visiting in winter, bring warm clothing, including a heavy coat, scarves, gloves, and a hat. The coastal areas can be particularly brisk due to the wind.

Activity-Specific Gear: If you plan specific activities like surfing or hiking, bring appropriate gear or research rental options in advance.

GETTING AROUND: TRANSPORTATION TIPS
Navigating through Devon, Somerset, and South West Cornwall can be an integral part of your travel experience. Each mode of transportation offers its unique perspective and set of advantages.

By Car

Flexibility and Reach: A car allows you to explore at your own pace and access areas that are off the beaten path. It's ideal for visiting remote beaches, country lanes, and hidden villages.

Driving on the Left: In the UK, driving is on the left-hand side of the road. It may take some getting used to if you're from a country where driving is on the right.

Narrow Roads and Lanes: Be prepared for narrow, winding roads, especially in rural areas. Some lanes are quite tight, requiring careful navigation and courtesy to other drivers.

Parking: In popular areas, parking can be limited. Check for designated parking areas and be aware of any parking fees.

Car Rentals: Numerous car rental agencies operate in the region. Book in advance, especially during peak tourist seasons.

Public Transportation

Trains and Buses: The regions are well-connected by rail and bus networks. Trains are great for covering longer distances quickly, while buses reach more remote areas not served by rail.

Planning Your Route: Utilize online resources and apps to plan your journey and check timetables. Be aware that services may be less frequent in rural areas and on Sundays.

Rail Passes: Consider investing in a rail pass if you plan to travel extensively by train. They can offer significant savings.

Local Tips: Don't hesitate to ask locals for advice on the best public transport options. They can often provide valuable insights.

Cycling and Walking

Scenic Routes: Both regions boast stunning landscapes ideal for exploring on foot or by bike. Coastal paths, moorland tracks, and country lanes offer a closer connection to nature.

Bike Rentals: Bikes can be rented from various outlets. Some areas also offer electric bikes for an easier ride.

Safety First: Always wear a helmet when cycling. Reflective clothing and lights are essential if you're out near dusk or dawn.

Walking Trails: There are numerous marked walking trails, ranging from easy strolls to challenging hikes. The South West Coast Path is a highlight for avid hikers.

Local Maps: Pick up local maps or download trail maps on your phone. They can provide information on route difficulty, distance, and terrain.

PART 2: DEVON – A COMPREHENSIVE EXPLORATION

INTRODUCTION TO DEVON

Welcome to Devon, a land where the lush greenery of the English countryside meets the majestic beauty of the sea. This corner of South West England is a embodiment of contrasts, where each thread weaves together to create a stunning and diverse landscape that is as rich in history as it is in natural beauty.

Devon is unique in boasting not one, but two distinct coastlines. To the north, you'll find rugged cliffs and wild, surf-lashed beaches that are a haven for adventurers and nature lovers alike. The south coast, on the other hand, is adorned with tranquil, sandy bays and picturesque estuaries, offering a more serene and gentle beauty.

Inland, Devon's charm lies in its rolling hills, hidden valleys, and the wild, untamed expanses of Dartmoor and Exmoor. These moors, with their wide-open landscapes and dramatic skylines, are steeped in mystery and folklore, inviting you to explore their many tales and natural wonders.

Devon is not just about its natural allure; it's also a place where history and modernity converge. Quaint villages with thatched cottages and medieval towns are interspersed with vibrant cities like

Exeter and Plymouth, offering a glimpse into the region's rich past while also providing all the conveniences and excitement of modern urban life.

As you journey through Devon, you'll discover a region that's passionate about its local produce. From fresh seafood caught off the coast to the rich dairy products from its pastoral farms, Devon's culinary scene is a delight for food enthusiasts. Cream teas, fresh scones with clotted cream and jam, and scrumptious pasties are just some of the local delicacies you must try.

Devon's culture is a celebration of tradition and creativity. From lively music festivals to quiet art galleries, from bustling farmers' markets to serene gardens, there's something here for every taste and interest.

As you explore this guide, you'll find detailed information about Devon's most famous sights, its hidden gems, and the best ways to experience all that this remarkable region has to offer.

KEY ATTRACTIONS

Valley of Rocks

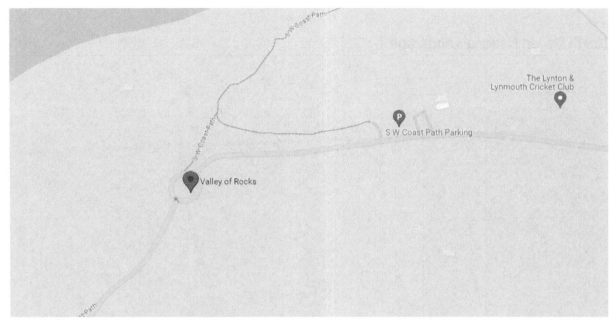

Location: Situated near the town of Lynton in North Devon, the Valley of Rocks is a renowned natural attraction along the South West Coast Path.

Description: The Valley of Rocks is celebrated for its dramatic and unusual rock formations, sculpted by centuries of weathering and erosion. This picturesque valley is fringed by towering cliffs and offers breathtaking views of the Bristol Channel. It's a geological marvel that draws visitors for both its natural beauty and its intriguing history.

Wildlife: One of the most unique aspects of the Valley of Rocks is its resident herd of wild goats. These hardy animals roam freely among the craggy landscape, adding a sense of wilderness and unpredictability to the area.

Historical Significance: The valley has a rich history, featuring in literature and folklore. It's thought to have inspired poets and writers like Samuel Taylor Coleridge and William Wordsworth. The dramatic scenery also makes it a popular location for filmmakers.

Activities: Ideal for walkers, photographers, and nature enthusiasts, the Valley of Rocks offers a range of walking trails with varying difficulty levels. The South West Coast Path runs through the valley, providing a scenic route for hikers.

Accessibility and Fees: The Valley of Rocks is open to the public year-round and does not require an entry fee. There are car parks nearby, some of which may charge a parking fee. The area is accessible by foot from Lynton and the neighboring village of Lynmouth.

Facilities: There are basic facilities available, including public toilets and a tea room in the vicinity. Picnic spots are also abundant, allowing visitors to enjoy the stunning views while dining al fresco.

Recommendations: Visitors are advised to wear appropriate footwear for rocky and potentially uneven terrain. Also, keeping a safe distance from the wild goats is recommended for both the safety of the animals and the visitors.

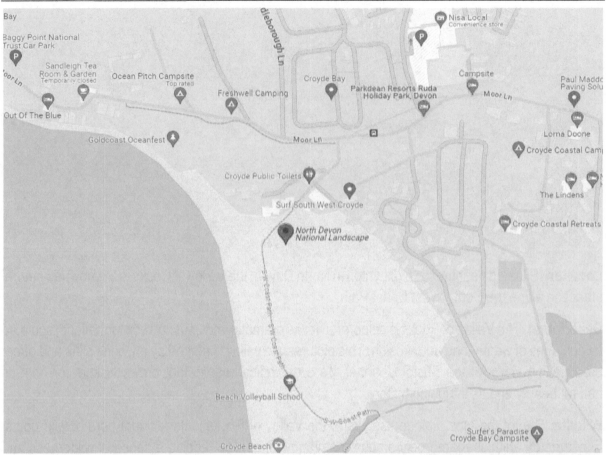

Stunning Coastal Scenery: The North Devon National Landscape stands out for its breathtaking coastal views, characterized by dramatic cliffs and beautiful sandy beaches. It's a natural spectacle that captivates photographers, nature lovers, and anyone seeking picturesque vistas.

Beach Paradise: This region is home to some of the finest beaches in Devon, including Woolacombe, Croyde, and Saunton Sands. These beaches are famous for their excellent surfing conditions, golden sands, and opportunities for various water sports.

Walker's Haven: A network of walking trails, including parts of the South West Coast Path, offers hikers the chance to explore the rugged beauty of North Devon's coastline. These trails provide both leisurely walks and more challenging hikes, each promising scenic ocean views and a connection with nature.

Rich Biodiversity: The area's diverse habitats, from coastal heathlands to maritime grasslands, are teeming with wildlife, making it a hotspot for birdwatching and nature observation. The variety of flora and fauna here is a testament to the ecological richness of the region.

Accessibility and Parking: There are multiple access points to the North Devon National Landscape, with parking facilities available near major beaches and trailheads. While access to the landscape is generally free, parking fees might be applicable in some areas.

Facilities and Amenities: Popular beach areas are equipped with amenities like cafes, restrooms, and lifeguard services during peak season. However, facilities might be limited in more remote locations, so it's advisable to plan accordingly.

Respect for Nature: Visitors are encouraged to respect the natural environment by adhering to conservation guidelines, staying on marked trails, and being mindful of the local wildlife and habitats.

Burrator Reservoir

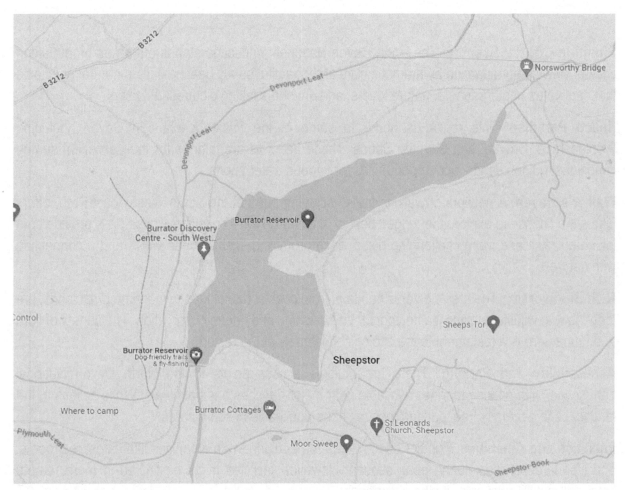

Scenic Walks and Views: Burrator Reservoir is renowned for its stunning natural beauty and serene environment. The area around the reservoir features a variety of walking paths that cater to all levels of hikers, from leisurely strolls to more vigorous hikes. These trails wind through picturesque woodlands and offer splendid views of the water and surrounding landscapes.

Wildlife and Nature: The reservoir is not just a favorite for walkers but also for nature enthusiasts and birdwatchers. The diverse habitats around Burrator Reservoir are home to various bird species and wildlife, making it a delightful spot for those interested in nature observation and photography.

Historical Significance: Besides its natural beauty, Burrator Reservoir has historical importance. It was constructed in the late 19th century to supply water to Plymouth, and the remnants of its historical infrastructure, like the old pumping stations, add an element of historical interest to the area.

Facilities and Picnicking: There are ample facilities for visitors, including parking areas and public toilets. The reservoir is also a popular spot for picnicking, with many visitors taking advantage of the tranquil setting for a relaxing day out.

Visitor Information: Burrator Reservoir is open to the public throughout the year, with no entry fee. It's advisable for visitors to check local guidelines for activities like fishing or boating if they wish to indulge in these during their visit.

The Milky Way Adventure Park

COSMIC TYPHOON
Minimum to ride 1.2m

ZIGGY'S BLAST QUEST
Minimum to ride 0.8m with an adult

GRAVITY RIDER
Minimum to ride 1 metre & 4 years old.
Maximum height of 2 metres.

COSMIC CATERPILLAR
Minimum to ride 0.8m with an adult

NINJA STARS
6 years+. Additional charge applies.

PLANET PLAY ADVENTURE PLAY AREA & SLIDES
Built for adults as well as children! Bare skin must be covered - nylon & polyester will burn on the slides.

LITTLE STARS
For children aged 0-6 years.

DROID DESTROYER DODGEMS
Min to ride 0.8m with an adult & 1.2m to drive

SCI-FI MEMORABILIA

JUMPING JUPITERS

THE MILKY WAY RAILWAY

MERLIN'S FAMILY SHOWS
6 days a week April-October. Select days during the winter

MAZE

POTTERY PAINTING
Pottery individually priced - but you take it home with you!

FANTASY FARM & BOUNCING BALLOON ROOM
Under 5's.

LASER TARGET SHOOTING
Suitable for older children & adults.

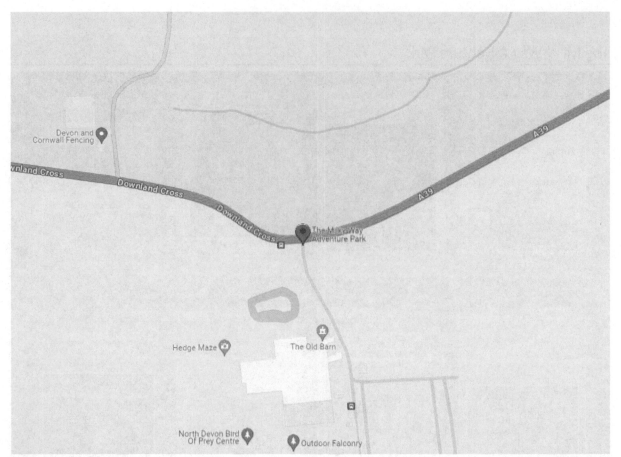

Family Entertainment: The Milky Way Adventure Park is a family-oriented amusement park that offers a wide range of attractions and rides suitable for all ages. From thrilling roller coasters to gentler rides for younger children, the park is designed to provide fun and entertainment for the entire family.

Indoor and Outdoor Activities: The Park features a mix of indoor and outdoor activities, making it a perfect destination regardless of the weather. Indoor play areas, shows, and exhibitions complement the outdoor roller coasters and adventure rides.

Special Events and Shows: The Milky Way Adventure Park is known for its entertaining shows and special events, which often include magic shows, live performances, and interactive experiences, adding to the park's appeal.

Dining Options: Visitors have various dining options within the park, ranging from snack bars and cafes to more substantial meal offerings. These cater to a variety of tastes and dietary preferences.

Opening Times and Tickets: The Park has specific opening times, which vary depending on the season, and it's recommended to check these in advance. There is an admission fee, and tickets can be purchased at the entrance or online, with options for day passes and season tickets. For more information visit https://www.themilkyway.co.uk/

Accessibility: The Milky Way Adventure Park is committed to being accessible to all visitors, with facilities and rides designed to accommodate guests with different needs.

Nestled in the picturesque Devon countryside, Buckland Abbey is a historic gem that tells a story spanning over 700 years. This former abbey, later converted into a house, was once home to the legendary sea captain Sir Francis Drake. Its rich history is palpable in every stone and artifact, making it a fascinating destination for history enthusiasts and casual visitors alike.

The Abbey is surrounded by lush gardens and woodlands, offering peaceful walks and a chance to enjoy the tranquility of the Devonshire landscape. The gardens themselves are a delightful mix of ornamental planting and productive orchards, providing a serene backdrop to the historical building.

Inside, Buckland Abbey houses a collection of artifacts and exhibits that give insights into its monastic past as well as its time as a private home. One of the highlights is the legendary Drake's Drum, said to beat in times of national crisis.

The Abbey also hosts a variety of events throughout the year, including historical reenactments, craft workshops, and family activities, making it an engaging experience for visitors of all ages.

Facilities at Buckland Abbey include a café serving locally sourced food and a gift shop offering a range of souvenirs and artisan products. There is an entry fee, with National Trust members enjoying free admission. Website: https://www.nationaltrust.org.uk/visit/devon/buckland-abbey

Dartmouth Castle

Overlooking the estuary of the River Dart, Dartmouth Castle has stood as a guardian of the town of Dartmouth and its strategic maritime position for over 600 years. This 14th-century fortress, combining both medieval and Victorian elements, offers a fascinating journey through the history of coastal defense.

Visitors to the castle can explore the old stone structure, climb the battlements, and enjoy stunning views of the Dart estuary and the sea. The castle's history is brought to life through various informative displays and interactive exhibits, detailing its role in defending the coast from potential invaders.

One of the unique features of Dartmouth Castle is its position at the mouth of the estuary, which can be enjoyed through scenic walks along the coastline or by taking a boat trip from the town quay.

The castle also boasts a café where visitors can relax and take in the views while enjoying light refreshments. Picnic spots are available in the surrounding area, making it a perfect spot for a leisurely day out.

There is an admission fee to Dartmouth Castle, with discounts available for families and groups. The castle is open to visitors throughout the year, though opening hours may vary according to the season.

Exmoor National Park

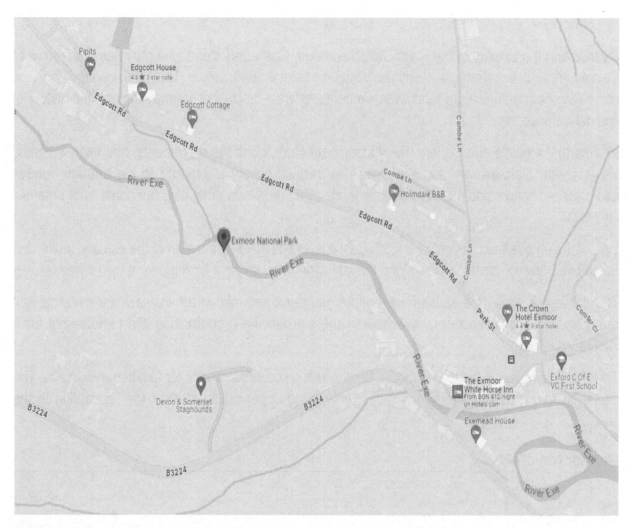

Exmoor National Park, a vast expanse of moorland, offers a stunning array of diverse landscapes ranging from rugged coastline to rolling hills and dense woodland. This natural paradise in Devon provides a sanctuary for wildlife and a playground for outdoor enthusiasts.

Visitors to Exmoor can immerse themselves in a multitude of activities. The Park is a haven for hikers, with numerous trails that meander through its varied terrain, offering breathtaking views and a chance to spot native wildlife like red deer and Exmoor ponies. For those interested in water sports, the park's rivers and coastline present opportunities for fishing, kayaking, and even surfing.

Exmoor's dark skies make it one of the best places in the UK for stargazing. The Park has been designated a Dark Sky Reserve, and on clear nights, the sky is alight with stars, providing an unforgettable experience for visitors.

The Park is also rich in history and culture, with ancient ruins, historic villages, and traditional pubs scattered across its landscape. These cultural hotspots offer a glimpse into the local heritage and provide a warm welcome to those exploring the area.

Entry to Exmoor National Park is free, and the park is accessible throughout the year. Facilities vary across the park, with visitor centers providing information, maps, and local tips to enhance your visit.

Paignton Zoo Environmental Park is a must-visit destination for animal lovers and families. Home to over 2000 animals across hundreds of species, the zoo offers an engaging and educational experience. From majestic African elephants to playful primates and exotic birds, the zoo provides an up-close look at wildlife from around the world.

The zoo's layout is designed to mimic natural habitats, giving visitors a sense of the diverse ecosystems these animals belong to. Informative talks and feeding sessions occur throughout the day, offering insights into the lives of the animals and the conservation efforts underway to protect them.

For children, the zoo is a place of wonder and learning. Interactive exhibits and play areas are scattered throughout the park, ensuring that the younger visitors are entertained while they learn about wildlife and conservation.

Paignton Zoo also hosts a variety of events throughout the year, from themed holiday celebrations to conservation talks and fundraising activities. These events add an extra layer of excitement to the zoo experience.

There is an admission fee to enter the zoo, with various ticket options available, including family passes and group discounts. The zoo is open year-round, but it's advisable to check opening times and any special events in advance. Website: https://www.paigntonzoo.org.uk/

Exeter Cathedral

Exeter Cathedral stands as an architectural marvel in the heart of Devon's capital city, Exeter. This magnificent cathedral, renowned for its stunning Gothic design, dates back to the 12th century and is one of the finest examples of Gothic architecture in England. The cathedral's most notable features include its two massive Norman towers and an impressive vaulted ceiling – one of the longest uninterrupted medieval vaulted ceilings in the world.

Visitors to Exeter Cathedral are treated to a wealth of historical and architectural wonders. The intricately carved facades, medieval stained-glass windows, and a beautifully ornate astronomical clock are just a few highlights that capture the essence of its historical grandeur.

One of the unique experiences offered by the cathedral is its rooftop tour. These guided tours take visitors up into the roof space and onto the rooftop, providing a unique perspective of the cathedral's architecture and breathtaking views over the city of Exeter.

The cathedral also hosts a variety of events throughout the year, including choir concerts, exhibitions, and educational tours, adding to its appeal as a cultural and historical hub in Devon.

An admission fee is required to enter Exeter Cathedral, with various ticket options available. The cathedral is open to visitors all year round, but it's advisable to check the schedule for any special events or services.

Powderham Castle, nestled in a picturesque setting near the Exe Estuary, is a historic estate with a rich history stretching back over 600 years. As the ancestral home of the Earl of Devon, the castle offers visitors a fascinating glimpse into the past, with its impressive architecture, beautiful gardens, and a captivating collection of art and antiques.

Guided tours of the castle provide an in-depth look at its history and heritage. These tours take visitors through grand state rooms, the medieval undercroft, and the Victorian kitchen, showcasing the lifestyle of its aristocratic inhabitants through the centuries.

The castle's grounds are equally impressive, featuring well-maintained gardens, a deer park, and scenic walking trails. The American Garden, the Rose Garden, and the Walled Garden are just some of the outdoor highlights that visitors can explore.

Powderham Castle is also a vibrant venue for events, including outdoor concerts, theater performances, and craft fairs, making it a lively cultural destination throughout the year.

Entry to Powderham Castle requires an admission fee, and visitors have the option of castle-only or grounds-only tickets, with family and group rates available. The castle and grounds have different opening times throughout the year, so it's recommended to check their schedule in advance.

Blackpool Sands, nestled in the South Hams area of Devon, is a renowned family-friendly beach, celebrated for its striking beauty and pristine conditions. This sheltered bay, with its turquoise waters and fine shingle beach, presents an idyllic setting reminiscent of the Mediterranean. Surrounded by evergreens and pines, it's a perfect spot for both relaxation and family fun.

The beach is well-equipped for a comfortable day out, with facilities including a café serving local and organic produce, showers, and toilets. For those looking to enjoy the water, there are opportunities for swimming, kayaking, and paddleboarding, with equipment available for hire.

Blackpool Sands is particularly noted for its commitment to environmental sustainability. The beach maintains high standards of cleanliness and water quality, making it a safe and appealing destination for families and nature lovers alike.

There's a parking area close to the beach, with a parking fee applicable. The beach is open year-round, but lifeguard services and facilities are typically available from May to September.

Dartmoor Zoo, set in the rolling hills of Dartmoor National Park, is a conservation and education center as well as a family attraction. The zoo is known for its efforts in wildlife conservation, especially for its collection of big cats, including tigers, lions, and jaguars.

Spanning 33 acres, the zoo provides a naturalistic habitat for its animals, aiming to educate visitors about wildlife conservation and animal behavior. Interactive exhibits and educational talks offer insights into the lives of the animals and the challenges they face in the wild.

The zoo gained fame with the publication of the book and the release of the Hollywood movie 'We Bought a Zoo,' which tells the story of how the zoo was saved by the Mee family. This story adds a unique personal touch to the visitor experience.

Facilities at the zoo include a café, picnic areas, and a play area for children. The zoo is accessible to visitors with disabilities, ensuring an inclusive experience for all guests.

An admission fee is required to enter Dartmoor Zoo, with various ticket options available. The zoo is open throughout the year, but opening hours may vary seasonally.

Credit: © South Devon Railway

The South Devon Railway offers a nostalgic journey back in time aboard a vintage steam railway. Running along the stunning River Dart between Buckfastleigh and Totnes, this heritage railway provides a unique way to experience the beautiful Devon countryside.

The journey on the South Devon Railway is a delightful experience, offering panoramic views of rolling fields, woodlands, and the river. The well-preserved steam locomotives and period carriages add to the charm, making it a favorite attraction for railway enthusiasts and families alike.

At Buckfastleigh, visitors can explore the railway's museum, gift shop, and café. The station is also home to a butterfly farm and otter sanctuary, offering additional attractions for a full day out.

The railway operates on selected dates throughout the year, with special events like Santa trains and themed journeys adding extra excitement to their calendar.

Tickets for the South Devon Railway can be purchased at the stations, with options for single, return, and all-day travel. Special rates are available for families, groups, and those looking to experience first-class travel. Website: https://www.southdevonrailway.co.uk/

HIDDEN GEMS

These attractions are less crowded, offering unique experiences or natural beauty that might not be as widely known.

Wheal Betsy

Wheal Betsy, tucked away in the Devon countryside, is a historic site that offers a glimpse into the region's rich mining past. The remains of this former silver-lead mine, including the striking engine house with its tall chimney, stand as a poignant reminder of the area's industrial heritage. This quiet and somewhat lesser-known site is perfect for those intere sted in local history and industrial archaeology.

Visitors to Wheal Betsy can explore the ruins and learn about the mining techniques and processes of the 18th and 19th centuries. Information boards around the site provide historical context, making it an educational experience as well as a scenic one. The surrounding landscape, with its moorland beauty, adds to the site's tranquil and reflective atmosphere.

There is no admission fee for Wheal Betsy, making it an accessible option for a peaceful exploration of Devon's history. The site is open all year round, and visitors can enjoy the surrounding walks and the picturesque views of the Tamar Valley.

Heddon's Mouth

Heddon's Mouth, situated in the Exmoor National Park, is renowned for its stunning natural beauty and offers some of the most amazing views in Devon. The area features a dramatic river gorge leading down to a pebble beach at the mouth of the Heddon River, where the rugged cliffs meet the sea.

The walking trails to Heddon's Mouth are among the highlights of the area, suitable for a range of abilities. These nature walks provide an opportunity to immerse in the lush woodland and coastal scenery, with the chance to spot local wildlife along the way.

The site is ideal for those seeking a tranquil nature retreat, with the sound of the river and the sea providing a serene backdrop. Picnic spots along the river and the beach make it a perfect location for a day out with family and friends.

There is no entry fee to Heddon's Mouth, and it is accessible throughout the year. Parking is available nearby, with a short walk leading to the main trails and the beach.

Hooken Cliffs

Hooken Cliffs, located near the village of Beer in South Devon, offer a spectacular coastal experience with breathtaking views. This area is known for its dramatic cliffs, formed by a significant landslip in the 18th century, creating an area of outstanding natural beauty with unique geological features.

The walking trails along Hooken Cliffs are less frequented, making them ideal for visitors seeking a quieter hike with stunning vistas. The paths wind along the cliff tops, providing sweeping views of the Jurassic Coast and the English Channel.

The area is a haven for birdwatchers and nature enthusiasts, with the cliffs and undercliffs supporting a variety of bird species and rare plants. The tranquil atmosphere and the natural beauty of the landscape make Hooken Cliffs a memorable destination for a peaceful walk.

Visitors can access Hooken Cliffs throughout the year without any admission fee. While the trails are not difficult, appropriate footwear is recommended due to the uneven and sometimes steep terrain.

Wistman's Wood

Wistman's Wood, nestled within Dartmoor National Park, is a mystical woodland known for its ancient, twisted oak trees, covered in a blanket of mosses and lichens. This ethereal woodland, with its gnarled trees and rocky terrain, seems to be straight out of a fairy tale and is steeped in local folklore and legends.

The woodland is a remnant of the ancient high-level woodlands of Dartmoor and provides a unique habitat for various wildlife, including rare lichens, birds, and insects. Walking through Wistman's Wood is like stepping back in time, with an atmosphere that is both enchanting and eerie.

The area is popular among walkers, nature photographers, and those seeking a spiritual connection with nature. The paths through the wood are uneven and can be challenging, so good walking shoes are essential.

Wistman's Wood is open to the public year-round with no entry fee. It's a relatively remote location, and visitors should be prepared for minimal facilities, ensuring they leave no trace to preserve the woodland's natural state.

Babbacombe Model Village

Babbacombe Model Village in Devon is a delightful attraction that captures the essence of English village life in miniature form. This unique attraction features hundreds of meticulously crafted models and miniature scenes that depict everyday life in an English village. The attention to detail in the models is extraordinary, showcasing quaint houses, gardens, and even tiny inhabitants going about their daily routines.

Visitors can stroll through this tiny world and appreciate the humor and creativity that have gone into creating each scene. The model village is not only a showcase of exceptional craftsmanship but also a playful and whimsical representation of village life.

In addition to the miniature models, the village includes beautifully landscaped gardens, adding to the charm of the experience. It's a popular attraction for families, photographers, and anyone with an appreciation for miniature art. Babbacombe Model Village is open throughout the year, with admission fees applicable. The village also features special illuminations and seasonal displays, making it a continually evolving attraction.

Watermouth Castle

Watermouth Castle, located near Ilfracombe in North Devon, offers a unique blend of history and entertainment. This Victorian-era castle, with its turrets and battlements, overlooks the picturesque Watermouth Cove. The castle has been transformed into a family-friendly attraction with a variety of theme park-style amusements and historical displays.

Inside the castle, visitors can explore rooms filled with Victorian artifacts and memorabilia, offering a glimpse into the past. The dungeons feature quirky and humorous displays that add an element of fun to the historical exploration.

The castle grounds are home to a variety of attractions including a water show, adventure playgrounds, and beautifully maintained gardens. The gnome land and fairy tale characters are particularly popular among younger visitors. Watermouth Castle is open seasonally with an admission fee. It's a perfect destination for families looking for a day out that combines historical interest with playful activities. Website: https://www.watermouthcastle.com/

Morte Point

Morte Point, a rugged headland on the North Devon coast, offers stunning coastal views and a sense of tranquility. This dramatic landscape, with its jagged rocks and steep cliffs, provides panoramic views of the Atlantic Ocean and the surrounding coastline.

The area is renowned for its wildlife, particularly seals, which can often be seen basking on the rocks below. The coastal walks around Morte Point are exhilarating, with the sea breeze and the sound of the waves adding to the experience.

The point is also steeped in maritime history, with tales of shipwrecks adding to its allure. The rugged beauty of Morte Point makes it a favorite destination for walkers, nature lovers, and photographers.

There is no admission fee to visit Morte Point, and it is accessible throughout the year. Visitors should be cautious when exploring the area due to the uneven terrain and steep cliffs.

Canonteign Falls

Canonteign Falls in Devon is home to England's highest man-made waterfall, set in a picturesque and tranquil setting. This breathtaking waterfall cascades down a sheer rock face, surrounded by lush woodland and serene lakes.

Visitors can take a walk up to the top of the falls and enjoy stunning views of the Teign Valley. The paths through the ancient woodlands and around the lakes provide a peaceful and relaxing experience, ideal for nature lovers and anyone seeking a break from the hustle and bustle of daily life.

The estate also features a children's play area, making it a family-friendly destination. In addition to exploring the falls and the surrounding nature, visitors can relax in the café, which offers a range of refreshments.

Canonteign Falls is open seasonally, with an admission fee to access the falls and the estate. The tranquil beauty of the area, combined with the impressive sight of the waterfall, makes it a must-visit destination in Devon.

Lydford Gorge

Lydford Gorge, the deepest gorge in the South West of England, is a natural marvel located on the edge of Dartmoor National Park. The gorge is renowned for its stunning waterfall – the Whitelady Waterfall, which cascades dramatically down a 30-meter drop. Alongside the waterfall, the gorge features a series of captivating nature trails that wind through the ancient woodland.

Visitors to Lydford Gorge can enjoy a scenic walk along the river, where they will encounter the enchanting Devil's Cauldron, a series of whirlpools and rapids that add to the area's mystical atmosphere. The gorge's lush environment is perfect for nature lovers and photographers looking to capture Devon's natural beauty.

Managed by the National Trust, Lydford Gorge offers well-maintained paths, although some sections can be steep and require sturdy footwear. Facilities at the site include a visitor center, a café, and a shop. There is an admission fee for access to the gorge, with National Trust members entering for free.

Greenway House

Greenway House, situated on the banks of the River Dart, is the beloved holiday home of the famous mystery writer Agatha Christie. This charming house, now managed by the National Trust, has been preserved as it was in Christie's time, offering a fascinating glimpse into the private life of the renowned author.

Visitors can explore the house, which is filled with Christie's personal collections, including family photos, first editions of her novels, and mementos from her travels. The house's interior and the surrounding gardens reflect the elegance and tranquility that Agatha Christie cherished. The gardens at Greenway are a particular delight, with their beautiful floral displays, woodland walks, and views over the river. The Boathouse, which features in one of Christie's novels, is another highlight of the estate.

Entry to Greenway House is ticketed, and visitors are encouraged to book in advance due to its popularity. Access to the house can be enjoyed by a ferry trip from Dartmouth, adding an extra element of adventure to the visit. Website: https://www.nationaltrust.org.uk/visit/devon/greenway

Tunnels Beaches

Tunnels Beaches in Ilfracombe, North Devon, offers a unique seaside experience with its hand-carved tunnels leading to sheltered bathing areas and tidal pools. Created in the 1820s, these Victorian tunnels provide an intriguing entrance to the beaches, which are set against a backdrop of rugged cliffs.

The beaches at Tunnels Beaches are renowned for their clear waters and safe bathing, making them ideal for families. The tidal pools are teeming with marine life, providing an opportunity for natural exploration and rock pooling.

Facilities at Tunnels Beaches include a café and a shop, and the site is also a popular venue for weddings due to its stunning coastal setting. There is an admission fee to access the beaches through the tunnels.

Bygones

Bygones in Torquay offers a unique step back in time with its life-sized recreation of a Victorian street. This immersive experience allows visitors to wander through a meticulously detailed Victorian era, complete with shops, a pub, and period homes.

The attraction is filled with thousands of genuine artifacts from the Victorian period, providing an authentic and educational glimpse into the past. In addition to the Victorian street, Bygones features a 28-foot model railway, a World War I trench, and various other exhibits that span different periods.

Bygones is a family-run attraction that appeals to all ages, offering an engaging and interactive way to learn about history. There is an admission fee for entry, and the attraction is open year-round.

Torcross

Torcross, located at the southern end of Slapton Sands in South Devon, is a tranquil coastal village known for its beautiful beach and serene environment. This less frequented spot offers a peaceful retreat with stunning views of Start Bay and a shingle beach that stretches for three miles.

The village of Torcross has historical significance, notably the Exercise Tiger memorial, commemorating the lives lost during a D-Day rehearsal that took place in the area during World War II.

Visitors can enjoy leisurely walks along the beach, explore the local wildlife at Slapton Ley Nature Reserve, or simply relax and enjoy the local seafood in one of the village's cafes or restaurants. Torcross provides a quieter alternative to the more bustling seaside resorts, making it ideal for those seeking a more laid-back coastal experience.

Shaldon Wildlife Trust

Shaldon Wildlife Trust, located in the picturesque village of Shaldon in South Devon, operates as a small, intimate zoo primarily focusing on the conservation of rare and endangered species. This compact sanctuary provides a unique opportunity to see and learn about a variety of animals from around the world, many of which are part of international breeding programs.

The zoo specializes in smaller animals, creating an intimate and close-up experience for visitors. From critically endangered primates to beautifully colored reptiles and birds, the Trust plays a crucial role in conservation efforts. Educational talks and feeding sessions offer insights into the lives of these animals and the challenges they face in the wild.

Shaldon Wildlife Trust is set in a lush, woodland garden, providing a tranquil setting for a leisurely visit. The zoo is committed to education and conservation, making it a valuable educational resource as well as a delightful visit for animal lovers of all ages.

There is an admission fee to enter the zoo, which directly contributes to their conservation work. The Trust is open throughout the year, but opening times may vary seasonally.

Ideford Common

Ideford Common, located near the village of Ideford in Devon, is a serene heathland habitat offering a haven for birdwatchers and nature lovers. This common land is known for its rich birdlife, where visitors have the opportunity to spot a variety of bird species in their natural habitat.

The common features a mix of heathland, woodland, and grassland, providing diverse environments for wildlife. It's an excellent spot for a peaceful walk, with well-marked trails that allow visitors to explore the area's natural beauty.

Spring and summer are particularly vibrant times to visit Ideford Common, with wildflowers in bloom and an active bird population. The common is also home to a range of other wildlife, including butterflies and insects, which thrive in the heathland environment.

Ideford Common is freely accessible to the public year-round, with no admission fee. Facilities in the area are limited, so visitors are encouraged to come prepared for a day in nature.

Hackney Marshes Local Nature Reserve

Hackney Marshes Local Nature Reserve, situated near the town of Newton Abbot in Devon, is a beautiful natural area that offers a peaceful retreat for wildlife and nature enthusiasts. The marshes provide a diverse range of habitats, including wetlands, grasslands, and woodlands, attracting a wide array of wildlife.

The reserve is particularly noted for its birdlife, with various species of waterfowl, waders, and songbirds. The marshes also support a variety of plant life, insects, and small mammals, making it a hotspot for biodiversity.

Visitors to Hackney Marshes can enjoy leisurely walks along the nature trails, where they can observe the wildlife and enjoy the tranquility of the reserve. The area is well-maintained with clear paths, and interpretive signs provide information about the local flora and fauna.

Hackney Marshes Local Nature Reserve is open to the public throughout the year and is free to enter. The reserve offers a wonderful opportunity to connect with nature and learn about the importance of wetland ecosystems.

Cockwood Harbour, located near Starcross in South Devon, is a picturesque coastal hamlet known for its idyllic scenery and abundant wildlife. The harbor, with its traditional fishing boats and yachts, offers a quintessentially English coastal experience.

The area around Cockwood Harbour is a haven for birdwatchers, as the tidal waters attract a variety of bird species. The serene environment and beautiful views make it an ideal spot for photography or simply enjoying a peaceful day by the water.

Cockwood Harbour is also renowned for its seafood, with local restaurants and pubs offering fresh, locally caught fish. The harbor's setting, with its charming cottages and tranquil waters, adds to the overall appeal of the location.

Accessible throughout the year, Cockwood Harbour does not require an admission fee. It's a delightful spot for those looking to enjoy the quieter side of Devon's coastline, with the opportunity to experience local wildlife and picturesque views.

ACCOMMODATION GUIDE

Please remember to confirm the prices and availability before making any reservations, as these are subject to change.

The Tree Inn (Approx. £45)
Address: Fore St, Stratton, Bude EX23 9DA, United Kingdom
A warm 3-star inn with bars, dining, free parking, breakfast, and Wi-Fi.

The Royal Hotel (Approx. £65)
Address: Barnstaple St, Bideford EX39 4AE, United Kingdom
Upscale 3-star hotel in a 17th-century building with free parking and Wi-Fi.

Premier Inn Exeter City Centre Hotel (Approx. £47)
Address: 2 Southernhay Gardens, Exeter EX1 1SG, United Kingdom
Modern, budget-friendly 3-star hotel with complimentary Wi-Fi.

Travelodge Exeter M5 (Approx. £34)
Address: Moto Service Area, M5 Motorway, Sandygate, Exeter EX2 7HF, United Kingdom
Modest 3-star hotel ideal for budget-conscious travelers, offering free Wi-Fi and parking.

Premier Inn Exeter Central St Davids Hotel (Approx. £47)
Address: Bonhay Rd, Exeter EX4 4BG, United Kingdom
Budget-friendly, air-conditioned 3-star hotel with Wi-Fi, near St Davids station.

Premier Inn Newton Abbot Hotel (Approx. £47)
Address: Greenhill Way, Kingsteignton, Newton Abbot TQ12 3SB, United Kingdom
Modern 3-star hotel with grill dining, free Wi-Fi, and parking.

Travelodge Paignton Seafront (Approx. £25)
Address: 3 Marine Dr, Paignton TQ3 2NJ, United Kingdom
Straightforward 2-star hotel with beach access and basic amenities.

White Hart by Marston's Inns (Approx. £50)
Address: 66 South St, Exeter EX1 1EE, United Kingdom
Storied 3-star inn with quaint rooms, a pub, free Wi-Fi, and parking.

The Railway Inn (Approx. £54)
Address: Queen St, Brixham TQ5 8BQ, United Kingdom
Known for comfortable accommodations and an on-site restaurant, offering free Wi-Fi.

Premier Inn Exmouth Seafront Hotel (Approx. £49)
Address: Esplanade, Exmouth EX8 2AZ, United Kingdom
Modern 3-star hotel opposite the beach, with free Wi-Fi.

Holiday Inn Express Exeter - City Centre (Approx. £57)
Address: Tudor St, Exeter EX4 3FL, United Kingdom
Unfussy 3-star hotel with free breakfast and Wi-Fi.

Southern Cross Devon Guesthouse and Tea Rooms (Approx. £63)
Address: High St, Newton Poppleford, Sidmouth EX10 0DU, United Kingdom
Warm 3-star guesthouse with a tea room, free breakfast, Wi-Fi, and parking.

Woodford Bridge Country Club (Approx. £37)
Address: Milton Damerel, Holsworthy EX22 7LL, United Kingdom
Rural 4-star hotel with a bistro, pool, spa, and free Wi-Fi.

The Devon Hotel (Approx. £66)
Address: Matford, Exeter EX2 8XU, United Kingdom

Modern 3-star hotel with bright rooms, gardens, free Wi-Fi, and parking.

Travelodge Okehampton Sourton Cross (Approx. £29)
Address: Sourton Cross, Okehampton EX20 4LY, United Kingdom
Modest 2-star budget hotel with free Wi-Fi and parking.

The Imperial Hotel (Approx. £41)
Address: The Esplanade, Exmouth EX8 2SW, United Kingdom
Victorian 3-star lodging with gardens, dining, free Wi-Fi, and parking.

OUTDOOR ACTIVITIES

Hiking and Walking: Devon's diverse landscapes provide numerous trails for both casual walkers and serious hikers. Explore the dramatic scenery of Dartmoor and Exmoor National Parks, or enjoy coastal walks along the South West Coast Path.

Beach Activities: With its extensive coastline, Devon is perfect for beach activities. Enjoy traditional seaside fun, swimming, rock pooling, or try your hand at surfing, particularly in North Devon, known for its excellent surf spots like Woolacombe and Croyde.

Cycling: Devon offers a range of cycling routes for all abilities, from gentle rides through picturesque villages to challenging off-road mountain biking in its national parks.

Water Sports: The county's rivers, estuaries, and coastline are ideal for water sports. Kayaking, canoeing, sailing, and paddleboarding are popular activities, with the River Dart being a particularly scenic spot for paddling.

Golfing: Devon boasts a variety of golf courses, from cliff-top links to parkland courses, catering to golfers of all skill levels.

Fishing: With both sea and freshwater fishing available, anglers can enjoy a range of fishing experiences in Devon. The rivers are known for trout and salmon, while sea fishing trips can be arranged from many coastal towns.

Horse Riding: Horse riding is a wonderful way to explore Devon's countryside. There are numerous stables and riding schools offering guided rides across moors, through woodlands, and along beaches.

Rock Climbing and Bouldering: The granite tors of Dartmoor provide excellent opportunities for rock climbing and bouldering enthusiasts.

Bird Watching and Wildlife Spotting: The diverse habitats in Devon, including wetlands, moors, and coastal areas, are great for bird watching and wildlife spotting. Key sites include the Exe Estuary and Lundy Island.

Gardening and Botanical Exploration: Visit the beautiful gardens spread across Devon, such as RHS Garden Rosemoor and the Lost Gardens of Heligan, to enjoy the lush, diverse plant life.

Adventure Parks and Zip-Lining: For a family-friendly outdoor adventure, visit one of Devon's adventure parks where you can enjoy zip-lining, high ropes courses, and other activities.

Stargazing: Areas like Exmoor National Park offer dark skies perfect for stargazing, with organized events and guided night walks available.

INDOOR EXPERIENCES

Museums and Galleries: Devon is home to numerous museums and galleries, showcasing everything from local history to contemporary art. Notable places include the Royal Albert Memorial Museum in Exeter, The Box in Plymouth, and the Bideford Museum and Art Gallery.

Historic Houses and Castles: Explore the grandeur of Devon's historic estates like Powderham Castle, Arlington Court, or the National Trust's Knightshayes Court. These venues often offer guided tours, giving insights into the local history and heritage.

Aquariums: The National Marine Aquarium in Plymouth is the UK's largest public aquarium and is a fantastic place to learn about marine life and conservation efforts.

Theatre and Performing Arts: Enjoy a play, musical, or dance performance at one of Devon's theaters. The Theatre Royal in Plymouth and the Northcott Theatre in Exeter are among the notable venues offering a variety of shows.

Food and Drink Experiences: Devon is famous for its local produce. Enjoy a traditional Devon cream tea, visit local breweries and wineries for tastings, or attend a cooking class to learn how to make regional specialties.

Wellness and Spa Retreats: For relaxation and rejuvenation, visit one of Devon's many spas. Indulge in treatments, relax in thermal pools, or enjoy a wellness retreat.

Indoor Markets and Shopping: Explore Devon's array of indoor markets and independent shops. The Exeter's historic quayside area, for example, offers unique shopping experiences with a range of artisanal products.

Cinema and Film: Catch the latest movies or independent films at Devon's cinemas. The county also hosts several film festivals throughout the year.

Indoor Sports and Leisure Centers: Stay active with indoor sporting facilities available in Devon, including swimming pools, climbing walls, and bowling alleys.

Escape Rooms and Indoor Games: For an exciting group activity, try one of the many escape rooms found in cities like Exeter and Plymouth, or visit an indoor gaming center.

Art and Craft Workshops: Participate in art and craft workshops, which are great for both adults and children. These can range from pottery and painting to textile work and jewelry making.

Libraries and Bookshops: Spend a quiet afternoon exploring Devon's libraries and bookshops, many of which host readings, author events, and book clubs.

DINING IN DEVON: WHERE TO EAT

Brasserie 16 at Devoncourt Hotel
Address: 16 Douglas Ave, Exmouth EX8 2EX, UK
Type of Meals: Offers a diverse menu in a warm and inviting atmosphere, perfect for both casual and special occasions.

Website: Brasserie 16
Devon Fish and Chips
Address: 1a Regent St, Teignmouth TQ14 8SJ, UK
Type of Meals: A classic choice for traditional English fish and chips, available for both dine-in and takeout, offering a quintessential British seaside dining experience.

The Devon Hotel
Address: Matford, Exeter EX2 8XU, UK
Type of Meals: Modern hotel dining featuring a range of culinary options, set in a hotel with bright rooms and beautiful gardens.
Website: https://www.devonhotel.co.uk/

Restaurant Twenty Seven by Jamie Rogers
Address: 9 Mill St, Kingsbridge TQ7 1ED, UK
Type of Meals: High-end dining experience focusing on local and seasonal ingredients, offering an innovative and contemporary menu.
Website:
https://www.restauranttwentyseven.com/

Devon View Restaurant at Highbullen Hotel Golf and Country Club

Address: Chittlehamholt, Umberleigh EX37 9HD, UK

Type of Meals: A fine dining experience offering exquisite dishes in an elegant and sophisticated setting, perfect for special occasions.

New Devon Takeaway

Address: 18 Ivydale Rd, Plymouth PL4 7DF, UK

Type of Meals: A great choice for traditional fish and chips, along with a variety of other takeaway options, ideal for a quick and satisfying meal.

Tyme Restaurant at Trimstone Manor

Address: Trimstone, Woolacombe EX34 8NR, UK

Type of Meals: Specializes in British cuisine with an emphasis on local flavors, particularly known for its delightful Devon cream tea.

Saveur

Address: 9 Tower St, Exmouth EX8 1NT, UK

Type of Meals: A cozy Modern European dining room offering a menu of innovative dishes, crafted with creativity and flair.

Website: https://www.saveur.co.uk/

Devon's Heaven's

Address: 5 Fleet St, Torquay TQ1 1BX, UK

Type of Meals: Although currently temporarily closed, this restaurant offers a range of dishes, appealing to a variety of tastes.

Rodean Restaurant

Address: The Triangle, Kenton, Exeter EX6 8LB, UK

Type of Meals: Known for its refined and innovative cuisine, this restaurant provides a cozy and intimate dining experience with a focus on quality and presentation.

Website: http://rodeanrestaurant.co.uk/

Trade Winds

Address: 12 Station Rd, Okehampton EX20 1DY, UK

Type of Meals: Offers a delightful range of traditional Greek dishes, perfect for those seeking authentic Mediterranean flavors.

Website: https://www.tradewinds.restaurant/

Horizons Restaurant

Address: South Devon College, Long Rd, Paignton TQ4 7EJ, UK

Type of Meals: This college-run restaurant provides a diverse menu, allowing patrons to enjoy a variety of dishes in an educational setting.

Devon Woodfired Pizzas

Type of Meals: Specializing in wood-fired pizzas, this eatery offers both dine-in and takeout options, perfect for pizza enthusiasts looking for authentic, rustic flavors.

Devon Larder

Address: 53 Queen St, Exeter EX4 3SR, UK

Type of Meals: A great spot for sandwiches and casual eats, ideal for a quick and satisfying meal with a convenient takeout option.

Hog Roast Heaven North Devon

1 Hoopers Water, Bideford EX39 4HE, UK

Type of Meals: Known for its hog roast and grill dishes, providing a hearty dining experience with both dine-in and takeout options.

The River Shack, Devon

Address: The Quay, Stoke Gabriel, Totnes TQ9 6RD, UK

Type of Meals: Offers a diverse menu with a focus on local produce, set in a picturesque location by the river.

Website: www.therivershackdevon.co.uk/

The Masons Arms, Knowstone

Address: Knowstone, South Molton EX36 4RY, UK

Type of Meals: Elegant and refined cooking in a picturesque thatched country inn, offering a fine dining experience.

Website: www.masonsarmsdevon.co.uk/

Devoncourt Resort & Apartments

Address: Douglas Ave, Exmouth EX8 2EX, UK

Type of Meals: Resort hotel dining that caters to a variety of tastes, set in a scenic location with multiple dining options.

Website: https://devoncourthotel.com/

Old Vienna Restaurant

Address: 7 Lisburne Square, Torquay TQ1 2PT, UK

Type of Meals: Offers a unique twist on modern cuisine with an Austrian influence, perfect for those looking for something different.

Website: https://oldvienna.co.uk/

LOCAL CULTURE & EVENTS

In the heart of the rolling hills and rugged coastlines of Devon, a calendar rich in tradition and modernity unfolds. Each year, the county bursts into life with an array of events and festivals that echo its heritage and celebrate its contemporary spirit.

As spring awakens the countryside, the Devon County Show, typically held in mid-May at Westpoint in Exeter, marks a celebration of Devon's rural heart. This event, one of the largest in the county, showcases the best of local agriculture, crafts, and cuisine. The air fills with the sounds of livestock, the sights of expertly crafted local goods, and the tantalizing aroma of Devonshire culinary delights.

Come late August, the historic port town of Dartmouth becomes a spectacle of maritime heritage during the Dartmouth Royal Regatta. Boats of all sizes race in the sparkling waters, while the skies are adorned with fireworks and air shows, bringing to life the town's nautical legacy.

Autumn brings a literary feast with the Appledore Book Festival. Nestled within the quaint village of Appledore, this event attracts authors, poets, and literary enthusiasts, turning the village into a hub of storytelling and literary discourse.

For art lovers, September is a month of exploration and discovery as Devon Open Studios allows a peek into the creative corners of local artists. Across Devon, studios open their doors, inviting visitors to witness the artistic process and perhaps find a unique piece to take home.

No exploration of Devon's culture is complete without indulging in its culinary heritage. The Exeter Food & Drink Festival, often held in late April or early May, is a testament to the region's rich food culture. Here, local produce, chef demonstrations, and food workshops come together in a celebration of taste and tradition.

A unique spectacle awaits in Ottery St. Mary on Guy Fawkes Night. The town's Tar Barrels event is an exhilarating tradition where brave locals carry flaming tar barrels through the streets, a sight that is both awe-inspiring and deeply rooted in the town's history.

Powderham Castle often steps back in time with historical reenactments. Medieval-themed activities, jousting tournaments, and historical demonstrations bring the past to vivid life within the castle's ancient walls.

The lush gardens of RHS Garden Rosemoor, not just a horticultural haven, play host to various events. From vibrant flower shows to garden festivals, the events here are a celebration of Devon's natural beauty and gardening prowess.

In the summer months, Devon's seaside towns twinkle with traditional seaside activities. From beach games in the sandy bays to sailing competitions in the blue waters, these activities are a nod to the county's enduring love affair with the sea.

Throughout the year, various towns and villages across Devon host craft fairs and workshops. These gatherings are a showcase of local craftsmanship, offering a glimpse into Devon's artisanal talents and an opportunity for visitors to learn a craft.

TAILORED ITINERARIES FOR DEVON

The Nature Lover's Journey (3-4 Days)

Day 1: Dartmoor National Park
- Begin with a day exploring the wild moors, granite tors, and ancient woodlands of Dartmoor.
- Enjoy hiking or horseback riding, and keep an eye out for Dartmoor ponies.
- Visit a local pub for a traditional Devonshire dinner.

Day 2: North Devon Coast
- Head to the North Devon Coast for breathtaking coastal walks.
- Visit the Valley of Rocks near Lynton and Lynmouth.
- Enjoy a seafood dinner at a coastal village like Ilfracombe or Croyde.

Day 3: Exmoor National Park
- Explore the diverse landscapes of Exmoor, from moorland to woodland.
- Visit the medieval village of Dunster and its castle.
- Stargaze at night in this Dark Sky Reserve.

Day 4: South Devon Beaches
- Relax at one of South Devon's beautiful beaches, such as Blackpool Sands or Bantham Beach.
- Optionally, visit the South Devon AONB for more scenic walks and quaint villages.

Cultural and Historical Exploration (3 Days)

Day 1: Exeter
- Start in Exeter, visiting its magnificent cathedral and Roman walls.
- Explore the Royal Albert Memorial Museum and the historic quayside.
- Enjoy dinner at one of the city's fine restaurants.

Day 2: Dartmouth and Totnes
- Visit the historic port town of Dartmouth. Explore Dartmouth Castle and enjoy a boat trip on the River Dart.
- In the afternoon, head to Totnes, known for its bohemian vibe and historic high street.
- Experience the local cuisine at a traditional Devon inn.

Day 3: Plymouth
- Explore the maritime heritage of Plymouth, including the historic Barbican and Mayflower Steps.
- Visit the National Marine Aquarium and Royal Citadel.
- End your day with a performance at the Theatre Royal or a meal at the Royal William Yard.

Day 1: Hiking in Dartmoor

- Tackle one of Dartmoor's many trails, such as the hike to Haytor Rocks.
- Visit a local climbing center for an afternoon of indoor climbing.
- Dine in a cozy Dartmoor pub.

Day 2: Cycling and Kayaking

- Cycle along the Exe Estuary Trail or the Tarka Trail in North Devon.
- In the afternoon, go kayaking or paddleboarding on the River Exe or River Dart.

Day 3: Surfing in North Devon

- Head to Woolacombe or Croyde for a day of surfing lessons.
- Explore the dunes at Braunton Burrows or relax on the beach.
- Enjoy a casual beachside dinner.

Day 4: Coastal Walking and Zip-lining

- Start with a morning walk along a section of the South West Coast Path.
- Spend the afternoon at an adventure park with zip-lining and high ropes courses.

FUN FACT: DEVON'S UNIQUE HERITAGE

The Tale of Two Coasts and Cream Teas: Devon is uniquely positioned in England with two separate coastlines — one on the English Channel to the south and the other on the Bristol Channel to the north. This geographical feature gives Devon a distinctive maritime heritage, with a history steeped in seafaring, fishing, and naval significance.

But it's not just the dual coastlines that make Devon stand out. The county is also famous for its contribution to one of England's most beloved culinary traditions: the cream tea. Devonshire cream tea, with its sumptuous clotted cream and jam on scones, is a matter of local pride and a subject of friendly rivalry with neighboring Cornwall. The debate over whether the cream or the jam should be spread first on the scone (Devon advocates for cream first, Cornwall for jam) is a playful and enduring aspect of this regional heritage. This culinary tradition is so deeply ingrained in Devon's culture that in 2010, the Devon Cream Teas were given Protected Designation of Origin status.

PART 3: SOMERSET & BATH – DISCOVERING THE HEART OF ENGLAND

INTRODUCTION TO SOMERSET & BATH

Somerset, located in the heart of South West England, is a county of stark contrasts and enduring charm. It's a land where lush green countryside meets historic towns, where ancient myths intertwine with a rich cultural heritage, and where every hill, valley, and village have a story to tell.

As you venture into Somerset, you are greeted by rolling hills and vast expanse of open moorland, notably the Quantock Hills and the Mendips, each offering breathtaking views and tranquil walks. The county is also home to part of the Exmoor National Park, an area of outstanding natural beauty, known for its dramatic coastline, heather-clad moors, and wooded valleys.

Somerset's history is as rich as its landscapes. The county is famed for its connections to King Arthur and the legends of Glastonbury. The Glastonbury Tor, a mystical hill topped with the remains of St. Michael's Tower, is steeped in Arthurian legend and offers panoramic views of the Somerset Levels. Below, the ancient town of Glastonbury, with its Abbey ruins and unique spiritual energy, draws visitors from around the world.

Bath, a World Heritage Site, is a jewel in Somerset's crown. Famous for its Roman-built baths and stunning Georgian architecture, Bath is a city that elegantly marries history with modern sophistication. The Roman Baths, Bath Abbey, and the Royal Crescent are testaments to the city's architectural and historical significance.

Somerset is also celebrated for its local produce and culinary offerings. The county is the birthplace of Cheddar cheese, made in the Cheddar Gorge, a spectacular limestone gorge renowned for its dramatic cliffs and subterranean caves. Somerset's cider is another hallmark of the region, with numerous cider farms dotting the countryside, offering tastings and tours.

Festivals and events are integral to Somerset's cultural fabric. The Glastonbury Festival, one of the world's most famous music and arts festivals, is held here. Additionally, the Somerset Carnivals, a series of illuminated processions through the towns, are a spectacle of light and creativity.

In Somerset, the arts are not just celebrated in festivals but also in everyday life. From the vibrant arts scene in Frome to the creative hubs in Taunton and Weston-super-Mare, the county is a haven for artists, craftsmen, and performers.

MUST-SEE SIGHTS & HIDDEN GEMS IN SOMERSET

Wookey Hole Caves

Address: The Mill, High St, Wells BA5 1BB, United Kingdom

Description: Wookey Hole Caves are a series of limestone caverns, a show cave, and tourist attraction in the village of Wookey Hole on the southern edge of the Mendip Hills near Wells in Somerset, England. The caves have been used by humans for around 45,000 years, evidenced by the discovery of tools and remains of animals such as hyenas and mammoths. Today, the caves blend their rich history with fun and educational tours, offering visitors a glimpse into both the geological and historical significance of the site. Attractions include the stunning cave formations, a life-sized dinosaur park, a 4D cinema, and mystical stories about the Witch of Wookey Hole.

Opening Hours: The caves typically open around 9:30 AM, but it's advisable to check the current opening times on their official website.

Website: https://www.wookey.co.uk/

The Bishop's Palace & Gardens

Address: The Bishop's Palace, Wells BA5 2PD, United Kingdom

Description: The Bishop's Palace has been the home of the Bishops of the Diocese of Bath and Wells for over 800 years. This stunning medieval palace, open to the public, is surrounded by a breathtaking moat with swans and contains a series of gardens that have been recreated to reflect various periods of the palace's history. The interior of the palace is equally impressive, showcasing historical architecture, the chapel, and rooms filled with art and artifacts.

Opening Hours: Generally opens at 10 AM, but it's best to confirm the current opening times on their official website.

Website: https://bishopspalace.org.uk/

Trull Waterfall

Location: Trull, Taunton, Somerset, United Kingdom

Description: Trull Waterfall, though lesser-known, is a charming natural feature near the village of Trull. It offers a picturesque and serene environment, ideal for nature enthusiasts and those looking for a peaceful spot. The area around the waterfall is suitable for short walks and provides a beautiful backdrop for photography.

Cadbury Hillfort

Location: Cadbury, Yeovil, Somerset, United Kingdom

Description: Cadbury Hillfort, often associated with the legendary King Arthur's Camelot, is an ancient hillfort offering panoramic views of the surrounding Somerset countryside. This historical site dates back to the Iron Age and provides a fascinating insight into ancient defensive structures. The hillfort is a popular destination for hikers and history buffs, with pathways leading around the site, allowing visitors to explore and appreciate the fort's historical significance and natural beauty.

Opening Hours: Accessible 24 hours, but visiting during daylight hours is recommended for safety and better visibility.

National Trust- Fyne Court

Address: Fyne Ct, Broomfield, Bridgwater TA5 2EQ, United Kingdom

Description: Fyne Court is a hidden gem nestled in the Quantock Hills. Once a grand estate, it is now renowned for its wild gardens and intriguing remnants of its past. The nature reserve offers a variety of walks through woodlands and parkland, often with musical and historical events taking place in the grounds. It's a perfect spot for nature lovers and families looking for an outdoor adventure.

Opening Hours: Open 24 hours, though visitor facilities like the tea room have specific timings.

Brean Down Fort

Location: Brean Down, Somerset, United Kingdom

Description: Brean Down Fort is a 19th-century fortification located at the end of a natural pier. This historical site offers stunning views of the Somerset coastline and the Bristol Channel. Visitors can explore the fort's remains, learn about its military history, and enjoy the surrounding natural beauty of the area. It's a perfect spot for history enthusiasts and walkers.

Burnham-on-Sea Beach

Location: 31 Esplanade, Burnham-on-Sea, Somerset, United Kingdom

Description: Burnham-on-Sea Beach is known for its long stretches of sand, iconic lighthouse on stilts, and family-friendly atmosphere. It's a great destination for traditional seaside activities like paddling, sandcastle building, and enjoying coastal walks. The beachfront is lined with shops, cafes, and arcades, making it an ideal spot for a leisurely day out.

Cheddar Gorge and Caves

Address: The Cliffs, Cheddar BS27 3QF, United Kingdom

Description: Cheddar Gorge and Caves, located in the Mendip Hills, are one of Somerset's most famous landmarks. The gorge boasts dramatic cliffs rising 450 feet, while the stunning stalactite caverns below are where Britain's oldest complete human skeleton, Cheddar Man, was found. Visitors can explore the caves, enjoy cliff-top walks, and learn about the gorge's prehistoric past.

Opening Hours: Opens at 10 AM; closing times vary seasonally.

Website: https://www.cheddargorge.co.uk/

National Trust- Dunster Castle and Watermill

Address: Dunster, near Minehead, Somerset, TA24 6SL, United Kingdom

Description: Dunster Castle is a former motte and bailey castle turned into a country house. Perched on a hilltop, it offers sweeping views of the Bristol Channel and Exmoor. The castle has a rich history spanning over 1,000 years, with beautifully preserved rooms and gardens. The adjacent watermill, dating back to the 18th century, is still operational.

Opening Hours: Opens at 10 AM; it is advisable to check the current opening times on their website.

Website: https://www.nationaltrust.org.uk/visit/somerset/dunster-castle-and-watermill

Ebbor Gorge National Nature Reserve

Location: Deerleap, Wells BA5 1AY, United Kingdom

Description: Ebbor Gorge is a lesser-known nature reserve offering a stunning landscape of woodland, limestone cliffs, and grassland. It's a fantastic place for hiking and wildlife watching. The gorge has several well-marked trails leading through diverse habitats, with breathtaking views and tranquil spots for nature observation.

Ninesprings Park

Address: Addlewell Ln, Yeovil, Somerset, United Kingdom

Description: Ninesprings is a delightful country park situated in the heart of Yeovil. It is renowned for its beautiful natural springs, scenic walking paths, and lush woodlands. The park is an ideal location for a leisurely walk, picnic, or simply to enjoy nature. With its abundant wildlife and picturesque settings, Ninesprings offers a peaceful retreat from the hustle and bustle of city life.

Opening Hours: The park is generally open from dawn to dusk, with the main gate closing around 6 PM.

Wells Cathedral

Address: Cathedral Grn, Wells BA5 2UE, United Kingdom

Description: Wells Cathedral is a stunning example of Gothic architecture and is famous for its magnificent West Front featuring over 300 statues and carvings. The cathedral's interior is equally impressive, boasting one of the oldest working clocks in the world and a striking "scissor arches" design. Visitors can explore the historical and architectural beauty of the cathedral, attend choral services, or simply enjoy the serene atmosphere.

Opening Hours: The cathedral usually closes at 6 PM, but it's advisable to check the latest opening times on their website.

Website: https://www.wellscathedral.org.uk/

Burton Pynsent Monument

Location: On the hill at Curry Rivel, near Langport, Somerset, United Kingdom

Description: The Burton Pynsent Monument is an 18th-century column located on a hilltop offering panoramic views of the Somerset countryside. The monument was erected in memory of Sir William Pynsent and stands as a testament to his contribution to the local area. Visitors can enjoy a scenic walk up to the monument and appreciate the surrounding landscape.

Access: The monument is open 24 hours and can be reached via a public footpath from the village of Curry Rivel.

Brean Beach

Address: Brean Down Rd, Brean, Burnham-on-Sea TA8 2RS, United Kingdom

Description: Brean Beach is a popular seaside destination known for its long stretch of golden sand, making it perfect for beach walks, sunbathing, and family activities. The beach is backed by impressive sand dunes and offers views of the historical Brean Down Fort. Visitors can also enjoy various amenities, including a cafe and nearby shops.

Notable Feature: The Victorian fort located at Brean Down, accessible by a walking trail, adds historical interest to the beach experience.

Burnham-on-sea Low Lighthouse

Address: River Parrett, Burnham-on-Sea, Somerset, United Kingdom

Description: The Burnham-on-sea Low Lighthouse is a distinctive structure standing on nine wooden piling legs on the beach itself. Built in 1832, it is one of the town's iconic landmarks and continues to function as a lighthouse. The unique design and scenic location make it a favorite subject for photographers and a must-visit for anyone exploring Burnham-on-Sea.

Opening Hours: The area around the lighthouse is open 24 hours, but access to the lighthouse interior is generally not available to the public.

Ashton Windmill

Address: Ashton Windmill, Chapel Allerton, Axbridge BS26 2PP, United Kingdom

Description: Ashton Windmill is a preserved 18th-century tower mill, set in the scenic Somerset countryside. It is a fine example of the windmills that were once common in the area, and it has been restored to working order. Visitors can explore this historic windmill, learn about its history and enjoy the picturesque surroundings.

Opening Hours: The windmill is open to visitors on select days, typically from 2:30 PM. It's advisable to check the latest visiting information before planning a trip.

Note: The opening times and days might vary, so it's recommended to verify the current schedule on their official or local tourism websites.

Museum of Somerset

Address: Castle Lodge, Castle Green, Taunton TA1 4AA, United Kingdom

Description: The Museum of Somerset, located within Taunton Castle, offers a rich journey through Somerset's history. The museum showcases a vast collection ranging from prehistoric times to the modern day, including Roman mosaics, Anglo-Saxon treasures, and exhibits on local industries. Interactive displays make it an engaging experience for all ages.

Opening Hours: The museum is open from 10 AM, but the closing times can vary. It's closed on Mondays.

Website: https://museumofsomerset.org.uk/

Brean Theme Park

Address: Leisure Park, Brean, Coast Rd, Burnham-on-Sea TA8 2QY, United Kingdom

Description: Brean Theme Park, located in Brean Sands, is Somerset's largest funfair. It offers a wide range of rides and attractions suitable for all ages, including roller coasters, water rides, and traditional fairground games. The park also has a variety of food outlets and entertainment options, making it an ideal family day out.

Website: https://www.breanthemepark.co.uk/

Hestercombe House & Gardens

Address: Hestercombe, Cheddon Fitzpaine, Taunton TA2 8LG, United Kingdom

Description: Hestercombe House & Gardens is a stunning historical estate boasting 50 acres of gardens designed by Sir Edwin Lutyens and Gertrude Jekyll. The gardens beautifully combine the formal and the informal, with water gardens, terraces, and woodland walks. The Georgian manor house also hosts art galleries and a café.

Opening Hours: Open daily from 10 AM, but it's best to check their website for the most current opening times.

Website: https://www.hestercombe.com/

National Trust- Lytes Cary Manor

Address: Lytes Cary, Manor near Somerton, Somerset TA11 7HU, United Kingdom

Description: Lytes Cary Manor is a charming medieval manor house surrounded by beautiful gardens and parkland. This intimate property offers a glimpse into centuries of family history and features a stunning Arts and Crafts garden with topiaries, herbaceous borders, and orchards.

Note: The property's opening hours can vary, and it's advisable to check the National Trust website for the latest information.

Ham Hill Country Park

Address: Ham Hill Rd, Stoke-sub-Hamdon TA14 6RW, United Kingdom

Description: Ham Hill Country Park is a vast nature reserve known for its rich wildlife and historical sites, including Iron Age and Roman remains. It offers panoramic views of the Somerset countryside, extensive walking trails, and areas for picnics and relaxation. The Park is a favorite for dog walkers, nature enthusiasts, and families.

Opening Hours: Open 24 hours, offering flexibility for early morning or evening visits.

Venus, Somerset Space Walk

Location: National Cycle Route 33

Description: The Somerset Space Walk is a scale model of the Solar System, with sculptures representing planets along the Bridgwater and Taunton Canal. The Venus sculpture is one of the installations on this unique trail, offering an educational and leisurely outdoor experience that combines astronomy with a scenic walk or cycle.

Somerset Fair

Location: Various locations in Somerset

Description: Somerset is known for hosting a variety of fairs throughout the year, celebrating local culture, arts, crafts, and food. These fairs often feature local vendors, traditional performances, and activities suitable for all ages. The specifics of each fair, including the Somerset Fair, can vary annually.

Blenheim Gardens

Address: Blenheim Rd, Minehead TA24 5QH, United Kingdom

Description: Blenheim Gardens is a beautifully maintained public park in Minehead. It features well-manicured lawns, vibrant flower beds, and a bandstand that hosts regular music events. The gardens provide a peaceful retreat for visitors and locals alike.

Opening Hours: Open daily until 8 PM.

Blake Museum

Address: 5 Blake St, Bridgwater TA6 3NB, United Kingdom

Description: Housed in a 16th-century home, the Blake Museum is dedicated to the history of Bridgwater and its surroundings. The museum's collections include archaeology, local history, and maritime history, offering insights into Somerset's rich past.

Opening Hours: Closed, but opens at 11 AM on Saturday.

Saturn, Somerset Space Walk

Location: 32H8+GX, along National Cycle Route 33

Description: Another installation on the Somerset Space Walk, the Saturn sculpture offers an interactive way to learn about the sixth planet from the Sun. This educational trail is perfect for families and school groups interested in astronomy and outdoor activities.

Animal Farm Adventure Park

Address: Red Rd, Berrow, Burnham-on-Sea TA8 2RW, United Kingdom

Description: Animal Farm Adventure Park is a family-friendly attraction featuring a variety of animals, play areas, and entertainment. The park provides opportunities for animal interaction, indoor and outdoor play, and seasonal events.

Opening Hours: Closed, but opens at 10 AM.

National Trust- Montacute House

Address: Montacute TA15 6XP, United Kingdom

Description: Montacute House is a magnificent Elizabethan mansion set in beautiful gardens. The house is known for its stunning architecture, historic collections, and landscaped gardens. Managed by the National Trust, it offers a fascinating glimpse into Elizabethan life.

Opening Hours: Closed, but opens at 10 AM.

Somerset Rural Life Museum

Address: Abbey Farm, Chilkwell St, Glastonbury BA6 8DB, United Kingdom

Description: This museum celebrates Somerset's rural and agricultural history. It's located at Abbey Farm and includes a farmhouse, a cowshed, and an apple orchard. Exhibitions showcase the county's farming heritage, traditional crafts, and rural community life.
Opening Hours: Closed, opens at 10 AM.

Website: https://swheritage.org.uk/somerset-rural-life-museum/

Wellington Park

Address: 3 Courtland Rd, Wellington TA21 8NT, United Kingdom

Description: Wellington Park is a beautifully restored Edwardian park with landscaped gardens, a bandstand, and a sensory garden. It's a popular spot for relaxation and hosts various community events throughout the year.

Opening Hours: Open daily until 7 PM.

Jupiter, Somerset Space Walk

Location: Liftknocker Cottage Coxhill

Description: Part of the Somerset Space Walk, the Jupiter sculpture is another educational installment along the Bridgwater and Taunton Canal. This model represents the largest planet in the Solar System and is part of the trail that scales down the solar system for a walking or cycling journey.

Mendip Hills National Landscape

Description: The Mendip Hills are designated as an Area of Outstanding Natural Beauty. This scenic landscape is famous for its limestone ridges, spectacular gorges, underground caves, and ancient sites. It's a popular spot for hiking, caving, and exploring the natural beauty of Somerset.

Open Hours: Open 24 hours.

Somerset Space Walk

Description: The Somerset Space Walk is a true-scale model of the Solar System along the Bridgwater and Taunton Canal. The trail features models of the planets placed at distances proportional to their positions in the Solar System, making it an educational and enjoyable outdoor experience.

Open Hours: Open 24 hours.

Somerset & Dorset Railway Heritage Trust- (Midsomer Norton South, Station)

Address: Somerset & Dorset Railway Heritage Trust, Silver St, Midsomer Norton, Radstock BA3 2EY, United Kingdom

Description: This volunteer-run railway heritage trust operates a short railway line and museum. Visitors can experience the history of the Somerset and Dorset Joint Railway, explore vintage trains, and sometimes enjoy a ride on a heritage steam or diesel locomotive.

Website: https://sdjr.co.uk/

RSPB Ham Wall

Description: Ham Wall is an RSPB nature reserve known for its remarkable array of birdlife, including rare species. The wetlands offer excellent birdwatching opportunities, walking trails, and beautiful views of the Somerset Levels.

Open Hours: Open 24 hours.

1 Strode House

Location: Near Barrington Court

Description: 1 Strode House, located near the historic Barrington Court, is part of a collection of properties that reflect the rural history and architecture of Somerset. It's a point of interest for visitors exploring the area's heritage and natural beauty.

Cheddar Gorge & Caves Car Park

Address: The Cliffs, Cheddar BS27 3QF, United Kingdom

Description: This car park serves visitors to Cheddar Gorge and Caves, one of the UK's most spectacular natural landscapes. The gorge is known for its dramatic cliffs, stunning stalactite caverns, and unique flora and fauna.

Open Hours: Open daily until 5 PM.
Website: https://www.cheddargorge.co.uk

Vivary Park

Address: Upper High St, Taunton TA1 3PY, United Kingdom

Description: Vivary Park is a historic and picturesque park located in the heart of Taunton. The park features a wide range of facilities, including a mini-golf course, a high ropes course, beautiful flowerbeds, and a café. It's a popular venue for events and a great place for family outings.
Opening Hours: Open daily, closes at 4:30 PM.

Website: https://www.somerset.gov.uk/locations/vivary-park-taunton/

West Somerset Railway- (Norton Fitzwarren, Station)

Address: West Somerset Railway, Norton Fitzwarren Station, Station Rd, Norton Fitzwarren, Taunton TA4 1BY, United Kingdom

Description: The West Somerset Railway at Norton Fitzwarren Station is part of the longest heritage railway in England. It offers a scenic journey through the Somerset countryside and coast. The station itself is a charming replica of a traditional railway station with a gift shop and café.

Website: https://www.west-somerset-railway.co.uk/

Avalon Marshes Centre

Address: Shapwick Road, Westhay, Glastonbury BA6 9TT, United Kingdom

Description: The Avalon Marshes Centre is situated in the heart of the Somerset Levels and Moors. It is a conservation area renowned for its rich birdlife and unique wetland habitat. The center provides educational displays, walking trails, and birdwatching facilities.

Opening Hours: Closed, opens at 10 AM.

Website: https://avalonmarshes.org/

Yeovil Country Park

Address: Addlewell Ln, Yeovil BA20 1QN, United Kingdom

Description: Yeovil Country Park is a large, green open space offering a variety of footpaths, scenic woodland walks, and a café. It's a great location for outdoor activities, wildlife watching, and leisurely strolls.
Opening Hours: Open 24 hours.

Grove Park

Address: 78 Upper Church Rd, Weston-super-Mare BS23 2DX, United Kingdom
Description: Grove Park is a delightful public park featuring landscaped gardens, a children's play area, and a peaceful pond. It's an ideal spot for relaxation and family-friendly activities.
Opening Hours: Open 24 hours.

Gough's Cave

Address: The Cliffs, Cheddar BS27 3QF, United Kingdom

Description: Gough's Cave, located in Cheddar Gorge, is famous for its stunning stalactite formations and underground river systems. It's one of the most significant natural wonders in the UK and offers guided tours that delve into the cave's geological and historical significance.

Opening Hours: Closed, opens at 10 AM.

Website: Cheddar Gorge - Gough's Cave

Westhay Moor National Nature Reserve

Address: Westhay Moor Drove, Westhay, Glastonbury, Somerset, UK.

Description: This nature reserve is a haven for birdwatchers and nature enthusiasts. It's known for its diverse bird species, particularly wetland birds, and its beautiful landscapes of reed beds and open water. Great for tranquil walks and wildlife photography.

Opening Hours: Open 24 hours.

Meare Fish House

Address: Porter's Hatch, Meare, Glastonbury BA6 9SR, UK.

Description: This historic building is a remnant of the monastic fishery that once served Glastonbury Abbey. It's one of the few surviving monastic fish houses in England and offers a glimpse into the medieval life of the area.

Opening Hours: Open daily until 5 PM.

Chalice Well

Address: Chalice Well Trust, 85-89 Chilkwell St, Glastonbury BA6 8DD, UK.

Description: The Chalice Well is one of Britain's most ancient wells, surrounded by beautiful gardens and orchards. It's a place of peace and spirituality, with the waters believed to have healing properties.

Opening Hours: Closed, opens at 10 AM.

Website: https://www.chalicewell.org.uk/

Seven Sisters

Description: The Seven Sisters are a series of rolling chalk cliffs along the English Channel. They are part of a stunning coastal landscape, offering breathtaking views and hiking opportunities.

Glastonbury Abbey

Address: Magdalene St, Glastonbury BA6 9EL, UK.

Description: The ruins of Glastonbury Abbey are steeped in history and legend, including ties to King Arthur. It's a site of archaeological significance and offers peaceful grounds for exploration.

Opening Hours: Closed, opens at 10 AM.

Website: https://www.glastonburyabbey.com/

East Somerset Railway- (Cranmore West, Station)

Address: East Somerset Railway, Cranmore West Station, Old Down Ln, Shepton Mallet BA4 4QP, UK.

Description: This heritage railway offers nostalgic steam train rides through the beautiful Somerset countryside. It's a great family attraction with special events and a museum.

Opening Hours: Open 24 hours.

Website: https://eastsomersetrailway.com/

Watchet Boat Museum

Address: Harbour Rd, Watchet TA23 0AQ, UK.

Description: This small museum located on Watchet's marina showcases the maritime history of the area with a collection of flatner boats and ot her nautical artifacts.

Opening Hours: Closed, opens at 10 AM.

Puxton Park

Address: Cowslip Ln, Hewish, Weston-super-Mare BS24 6AH, UK.

Description: Puxton Park is an adventure and farm animal park offering a variety of outdoor activities. It has play areas, animal encounters, and indoor fun for all ages, making it an ideal family destination.

Opening Hours: Open daily, closes at 5:30 PM.

Website: https://www.puxton.co.uk/

East Somerset Railway- (Merryfield Lane, Station)

Address: Merryfield Lane Station, East Somerset Railway, No Road Access, off Merryfield Ln, Somerset, UK.

Description: This part of the East Somerset Railway offers a quaint and nostalgic train journey experience. It's a chance to enjoy the beautiful Somerset countryside aboard historic steam trains.

Opening Hours: Open 24 hours.

French Weir Park

Address: 15 Northfield Ave, Taunton TA1 1XF, UK.

Description: French Weir Park is a riverside park that features a playground and a variety of open spaces. It's perfect for family outings, with areas for children to play and paths for tranquil walks.

Website: French Weir Park

Shepton Mallet Prison

Address: Frithfield Ln, Shepton Mallet BA4 5LU, UK.

Description: This former prison now offers guided tours, ghost hunts, and historical insights into prison life. It's a unique and eerie attraction for those interested in historical and paranormal activities.

Opening Hours: Closed, opens at 10 AM.

Website: https://sheptonmalletprison.com/

Chard Museum

Address: Godworthy House, High St, Chard TA20 1QB, UK.
Description: Chard Museum showcases the local history and heritage of Chard and the surrounding area. It includes displays on local industries, historical artifacts, and more.
Opening Hours: Closed, opens at 10 AM on Wednesday.
Website: https://www.chardmuseum.co.uk/

Somerset Aerofest (Middlezoy Aerodrome)

Address: Middlezoy, Somerset, UK.

Description: Somerset Aerofest is an aviation event held at Middlezoy Aerodrome, showcasing a variety of aircraft and aerial displays. It's a celebration of aviation history and a great event for enthusiasts.

Landacre Bridge

Address: Landacre Ln, Withypool, Minehead TA24 7TT, UK.

Description: Landacre Bridge, located in Exmoor National Park, is a picturesque medieval bridge. It's a peaceful spot, ideal for picnics, walks, and enjoying the natural beauty of the surroundings.
Opening Hours: Open 24 hours.

Knightstone Island

Address: Knightstone Beacon, Knightstone Causeway, Weston-super-Mare, UK.

Description: Knightstone Island is a historic island connected by a causeway, offering scenic views, a theatre, and cafes. It's a great place for a leisurely walk and to soak in the maritime atmosphere.

Catcott Complex Nature Reserve

Address: West Drove, Near Burtle, (also close to Catcott), Somerset, UK.

Description: This nature reserve is a haven for wildlife, particularly birds. It features diverse habitats including wetlands and woodlands, making it a prime spot for birdwatching and nature walks.

Opening Hours: Open, closes at 7 PM.

MUST-SEE SIGHTS & HIDDEN GEMS IN BATHS

The Roman Baths

Address: Abbey Churchyard, Bath BA1 1LZ, United Kingdom.
Features: The Roman Baths is one of the most well-preserved Roman remains in the world. This historic site features the ancient Roman bathing complex, a museum displaying Roman artifacts, and the Pump Room restaurant. The baths themselves are below the modern street level and include the Sacred Spring, the Roman Temple, the Roman Bath House, and finds from Roman Bath.
Opening Hours: Varies seasonally. It's recommended to check their website for current timings.
Website: https://www.romanbaths.co.uk/

Bath Skyline

Features: The Bath Skyline offers a picturesque 6-mile trail that provides stunning panoramic views of the city of Bath. This trail is popular for walking, running, and enjoying nature. It circles the city and takes in meadows, woodlands, and historic sites, offering a unique perspective of Bath's urban and rural landscapes.

Pulteney Bridge

Address: Bridge St, Bath BA2 4AT, United Kingdom.
Features: Pulteney Bridge is one of the few bridges in the world lin ed with shops. Built in the 18th century, it crosses the River Avon and is notable for its beautiful Georgian architecture. It's a great spot for photography and offers a charming view of the river and city.

Royal Victoria Park

Address: Marlborough Ln, Bath BA1 2NQ, United Kingdom.
Features: Opened in 1829, Royal Victoria Park is a large public park with expansive lawns, a botanical garden, and a bandstand. It's a perfect place for picnics, leisurely walks, and enjoying outdoor events. The Park is especially known for its stunning views of the Royal Crescent.

The Holburne Museum

Address: Great Pulteney St, Bath BA2 4DB, United Kingdom.
Features: The Holburne Museum houses a fine collection of art and silver from the Victorian era. It's set in a historic 18th-century building at the end of Great Pulteney Street. The museum's collection includes works by Gainsborough, Guardi, Stubbs, and Turner, and it hosts a range of temporary exhibitions.

Sham Castle

Address: Golf Course Rd, Bath BA2 6JG, Unite d Kingdom.

Features: Sham Castle is a folly built around 1755, situated on the Bath Golf Club's grounds. It's a striking example of a mock castle, and though only the front wall exists, it creates a picturesque view, especially when lit up at night.

Bath Abbey

Features: Bath Abbey is a stunning example of Perpendicular Gothic architecture. It's known for its fan vaulting, magnificent stained glass windows, and its role as a central place of Christian worship for over a thousand years. The Abbey stands at the heart of Bath and offers visitors a rich historical experience.

Thermae Bath Spa

Address: The Hetling Pump Room, Hot Bath St, Bath BA1 1SJ, United Kingdom.

Features: The Thermae Bath Spa is a blend of historic and contemporary, offering a range of spa facilities including thermal baths fed by natural hot springs, a rooftop pool with stunning city views, and various steam rooms and therapies. It's a unique place to relax and rejuvenate in the only naturally warm, mineral-rich waters in Britain.

National Trust- Bath Assembly Rooms

Address: Bennett St, Bath BA1 2QH, United Kingdom.

Features: The Bath Assembly Rooms, managed by the National Trust, were a social hub of Georgian high society. The rooms are elegantly decorated and include the famous Ball Room, the Tea Room, and the Card Room. They offer a glimpse into the luxurious lifestyle of the 18th century.

Royal Crescent

Address: The Royal Crescent, Royal Cres, Bath BA1 2LR, United Kingdom.

Features: The Royal Crescent is one of Bath's most iconic landmarks, featuring a sweeping curve of 30 Grade I listed terrace houses. It's a fine example of Georgian architecture, designed by John Wood the Younger and built between 1767 and 1774.

Victoria Art Gallery

Address: Bridge St, Bath BA2 4AT, United Kingdom.

Features: The Victoria Art Gallery houses an impressive collection of British and European art. The gallery showcases paintings, sculpture, and decorative arts, with works from artists like Gainsborough and Turner. It also hosts temporary exhibitions.

Kensington Meadows

Address: 183 Ringswell Gardens, Bath BA1 6TT, United Kingdom.

Features: Kensington Meadows is a serene green space near the River Avon, offering a peaceful retreat from the city's bustle. It's ideal for walks, picnics, and enjoying the natural environment.

The Circus

Features: The Circus in Bath is a notable example of Georgian architecture. Comprising three long, curved terraces, it's designed to form a circle and is known for its striking façade, intricate stone carvings, and historical significance.

Botanical Gardens

Address: Park Ln, Bath BA1 3EF, United Kingdom.

Features: The Botanical Gardens in Bath are part of Royal Victoria Park and feature a diverse range of plants and flowers. The gardens have a romantic and historic feel, with various sections including a rockery, herbaceous borders, and a scented walk.

Henrietta Park

Address: Henrietta Rd, Bath BA2 6LX, United Kingdom.

Features: Henrietta Park is a historic green space offering a calm and peaceful environment. It's well-maintained with beautiful flower beds, walking paths, and open spaces, making it perfect for relaxation and leisurely strolls.

The Gravel Walk

Address: 1-2 Queen's Parade Pl, Bath BA1 2NR, United Kingdom.

Features: The Gravel Walk is a historic pathway in Bath, popular for its picturesque scenery. It's known for being a romantic walking route and features in Jane Austen's novel 'Persuasion'. The walk offers a charming experience amidst the city's Georgian architecture.

The Jane Austen Centre

Address: 40 Gay St, Bath BA1 2NT, United Kingdom.

Features: This museum is dedicated to the life and works of the renowned author Jane Austen, who lived in Bath in the early 19th century. The centre offers insights into her life, the Regency period, and how the city influenced her writing.

Bath Deep Lock (8/9)

Address: Pulteney Rd (South), Bath BA2 4AX, United Kingdom.

Features: Bath Deep Lock is one of the deepest canal locks in the UK. It's an interesting spot for engineering enthusiasts and those interested in the canal history of Bath.

The Giant Plane Tree

Address: Elton House, Abbey St, Bath BA1 1EE, United Kingdom.
Features: The Giant Plane Tree is known for its remarkable size and age. It's a significant natural landmark in Bath and provides a striking example of the city's greenery.

Palladian Bridge

Features: The Palladian Bridge in Bath is an elegant and architecturally significant bridge, designed in the Palladian style. It's a picturesque spot often visited for its serene beauty and historical significance.

Devonshire Tunnel (Western Portal)

Address: 10 Egerton Rd, Bath BA2 4AD, United Kingdom.
Features: The Devonshire Tunnel is part of the Two Tunnels Greenway cycling and walking route. The Western Portal offers an interesting glimpse into t he city's railway history, now repurposed for recreational use.

The Museum of East Asian Art

Address: 12 Bennett St, Bath BA1 2QJ, United Kingdom.

Features: This museum houses a fine collection of East Asian art and artefacts, including Chinese, Japanese, Korean, and Southeast Asian pieces. It's a window into the rich artistic traditions of East Asia.

Museum of Bath at Work

Address: Julian Rd, Bath BA1 2RH, United Kingdom.

Features: The museum presents the industrial heritage of Bath, displaying replica workplaces and exhibitions that illustrate the city's working history.

Mary Shelley's House of Frankenstein

Address: 37 Gay St, Bath BA1 2NT, United Kingdom.

Features: This attraction is dedicated to Mary Shelley and her most famous creation, 'Frankenstein'. It's a unique experience, blending horror, history, and literature.

The Bath Lookout

Address: 56 Alexandra Park, Shakespeare Ave, Bath BA2 4RQ, United Kingdom.

Features: The Bath Lookout offers panoramic views of the city. It's a popular spot for visitors and locals alike, providing a spectacular vantage point over Bath.

Kelston Roundhill

Features: Kelston Roundhill is known for its scenic walking path and breathtaking views of the surrounding countryside. It's a perfect spot for nature lovers and hikers.

Warleigh Weir

Address: Ferry Ln, Claverton, Bath BA2 7BH, United Kingdom.

Features: Warleigh Weir is a picturesque spot on the River Avon, popular for swimming and picnics. It's a beautiful natural setting close to the city.

Georgian Garden

Features: The Georgian Garden in Bath is a restored 18th-century garden, offering a glimpse into the gardening style of the Georgian era. It's a peaceful retreat within the city.

Avoncliff Aqueduct

Address: Canal Cottage, Dundas Aqueduct, Bath BA15 2JH, United Kingdom.

Features: The Avoncliff Aqueduct carries the Kennet and Avon Canal over the River Avon and is a fine example of Georgian engineering. It's a popular spot for walking and cycling.

Bizarre Bath

Address: Terrace Walk, Bath BA1 1LN, United Kingdom.

Features: Bizarre Bath is a unique evening entertainment experience that combines comedy with a walking tour, showcasing a different and humorous side of Bath.

Parade Gardens

Address: Grand Parade, Bath BA2 4DF, United Kingdom.

Features: These beautifully maintained gardens offer a stunning view of Pulteney Bridge and the River Avon. They're known for their floral displays and are a popular spot for relaxation in the city center.

National Trust- Prior Park Landscape Garden

Address: Ralph Allen Dr, Bath BA2 5AH, United Kingdom.

Features: This 18th-century landscape garden offers breathtaking views over the city of Bath. It features one of only four Palladian bridges in the world and is renowned for its serene beauty.

The Great Dell

Address: Royal Victoria Park, Bath BA1 2NR, United Kingdom.

Features: The Great Dell is a secluded and wooded area within Royal Victoria Park, offering a quiet escape from the city's hustle and bustle. It's known for its collection of trees and peaceful atmosphere.

City Sightseeing Bath Hop On Hop Off

Address: 6 N Parade, Bath BA1 1LF, United Kingdom.

Features: This tour service offers a convenient way to explore Bath's main attractions. The hop-on hop-off buses provide commentary, giving insights into the city's rich history and culture.

Combe Down Tunnel (Northern Portal)

Address: Cotswold, Perrymead, Bath BA2 5JR, United Kingdom.

Features: The Northern Portal of the Combe Down Tunnel is part of the Two Tunnels Greenway. It's the UK's longest cycling and walking tunnel, offering a unique experience.

Combe Down Tunnel (Southern Portal)

Address: Two Tunnels Greenway, Bath BA2 5AH, United Kingdom.

Features: The Southern Portal marks the other end of the Combe Down Tunnel. The tunnel features an interactive light and sound installation, enhancing the experience of visitors.

Sydney Gardens

Address: Sydney Pl, Bath BA2 6NT, United Kingdom.

Features: Sydney Gardens is Bath's oldest park and was a favorite spot of Jane Austen. It's known for its historical importance and offers a pleasant environment for walks and relaxation.

Geo Dome Structure

Address: Great Pulteney St, Bath BA2 4BU, United Kingdom.

Features: The Geo Dome Structure is a modern architectural feature in Bath, offering an interesting visual contrast to the city's predominantly Georgian architecture. It's a distinctive landmark and photo opportunity.

Bath Ghost Tours

Address: Abbey Churchyard, Bath, United Kingdom.

Features: Bath Ghost Tours offer a spooky and entertaining insight into Bath's haunted history. These evening walking tours are led by knowledgeable guides and take visitors to some of the city's most ghostly locations.

Angel of Peace

Address: Parade Gardens, Bath, United Kingdom.

Features: The Angel of Peace is a notable statue located in the picturesque Parade Gardens. It's a beautiful and serene spot overlooking the River Avon, ideal for relaxation and contemplation.

Alexandra Park

Address: Shakespeare Ave, Bath BA2 4RQ, United Kingdom.

Features: Alexandra Park offers some of the best panoramic views of Bath. It's a perfect place for a leisurely walk, picnic, or simply to enjoy the scenic overlook of the city.

Brickfields Park

Address: 1A The Hollow, Bath BA2 1LZ, United Kingdom.

Features: Brickfields Park is a small but charming community park. It's a great spot for families and includes play areas for children.

Millennium Viewpoint

Address: The West Barn, Manor Farm Buildings, Bath, United Kingdom.
Features: The Millennium Viewpoint provides a unique vantage point for visitors to enjoy sweeping views of the surrounding area. It's a hidden gem for those who love scenic spots.

Avon Towpath

Features: The Avon Towpath runs along the River Avon and offers a peaceful walking and cycling route. It's popular for its beautiful riverside scenery and wildlife.

Bath Pumpkin Patch

Address: Newbridge Rd, Bath, United Kingdom.
Features: Bath Pumpkin Patch is a seasonal attraction that offers a fun family experience. Visitors can pick their own pumpkins and enjoy the autumnal atmosphere.

Alice Park

Address: Gloucester Rd, Bath BA1 6EE, United Kingdom.
Features: Alice Park is a community park with a café, children's play area, and tennis courts. It's a lovely spot for families and those seeking a quiet green space.

Weston Lock

Address: 22 Brassmill Ln, Bath BA1 3JW, United Kingdom.
Features: Weston Lock is part of the Kennet and Avon Canal system and offers a glimpse into the historic waterways of Bath. It's an interesting spot for those fascinated by industrial heritage.

St Stephen's Millennium Green

Address: Richmond Rd, Bath BA1 3ER, United Kingdom.
Features: St Stephen's Millennium Green is a small urban park that provides a tranquil green space in the city. It's a nice place for a leisurely stroll or a quiet moment.

Prince Bladud and the Pig

Address: Grand Parade, Bath, United Kingdom.
Features: This sculpture is a tribute to Prince Bladud, a legendary figure who, according to myth, founded the city of Bath. The sculpture adds a whimsical touch to the Grand Parade area.

Beckford's Tower and Museum

Address: Lansdown Rd, Bath BA1 9BH, United Kingdom.
Features: Beckford's Tower is a remarkable neoclassical tower, once a retreat for William Beckford, a famous writer and collector. The museum inside showcases his life and works.

Laura Place Fountain

Address: Laura Pl, Bath BA2 4BJ, United Kingdom.
Features: The Laura Place Fountain is an elegant historic fountain located in a picturesque square. It's a charming spot, often admired for its Georgian architecture.

Steep Walk to Alexandra Park

Address: 13 Alexandra Rd, Bath BA2 4PW, United Kingdom.
Features: The steep walk to Alexandra Park is a bit challenging but rewards visitors with stunning views of Bath from the top. It's a popular spot for walkers and photographers.

National Trust- Dyrham Park

Features: Dyrham Park is a baroque country house set in an ancient deer park. It offers visitors a glimpse into 17th-century life with its opulent interiors and beautiful gardens.

Somersetshire Coal Canal

Features: The Somersetshire Coal Canal is a part of the region's industrial heritage. While no longer in use, parts of the canal are still visible and make for an interesting historical visit.

National Trust- Bath Skyline

Address: Kent House, Ralph Allen Dr, Bath BA2 5AH, United Kingdom.
Features: The Bath Skyline walk provides breathtaking views of the city and its surroundings. It's a popular walking route for locals and visitors alike, offering a chance to experience the natural beauty of the area.

Victoria Bridge, Bath

Address: 75-76 Victoria Bridge Rd, Bath BA2 3ET, United Kingdom.
Features: Victoria Bridge is a historic bridge over the River Avon. It's a fine example of 19th-century engineering and a picturesque spot for a leisurely walk.

Sir Bevil Grenville's Monument

Address: Cotswold Way, near Bath, United Kingdom.
Features: This monument commemorates Sir Bevil Grenville, a Royalist commander in the English Civil War. It stands as a testament to his bravery and is located at the site of the Battle of Lansdowne.

Bath World Heritage Centre

Address: 10 York St, Bath BA1 1NG, United Kingdom.
Features: The Bath World Heritage Centre provides insights into why Bath has been designated a UNESCO World Heritage Site. It's an educational resource that highlights the city's unique cultural and historical significance.

Memorial to Admiral Arthur Phillip

Address: Bennett St, Bath, United Kingdom.

Features: This memorial honors Admiral Arthur Phillip, the first Governor of New South Wales and the founder of the modern Australian city of Sydney. It is a tribute to his significant historical contributions.

Theatre Royal, Bath

Address: Saw Cl, Bath BA1 1EY, United Kingdom.

Features: The Theatre Royal is one of the oldest and most beautiful theatres in Britain. It hosts a variety of performances, from traditional plays to modern acts, offering a rich cultural experience.

Bathwick Meadow

Features: Bathwick Meadow is a serene green space offering picturesque views and a quiet escape from the city. It's ideal for leisurely walks and enjoying the natural surroundings.

Sally Lunn's Historic Eating House & Museum

Address: 4 North Parade Passage, Bath BA1 1NX, United Kingdom.

Features: Sally Lunn's is one of the oldest houses in Bath, now serving as a charming tea house and museum. It's famous for the Sally Lunn Bun, a local delicacy with historical significance.

Primrose Hill Community Woodland

Address: 1 Fonthill Rd, Bath BA1 5RH, United Kingdom.

Features: This community woodland offers a tranquil environment for nature walks. It's a great place to enjoy the local flora and fauna.

Hen Weekends in Bath

Address: Beau Nash House, 19 Union Passage, Bath BA1 1RD, United Kingdom.

Features: Hen Weekends in Bath specializes in organizing memorable hen parties and events, offering a range of activities tailored to groups visiting Bath for special occasions.

Best of Bath Walking Tours

Address: Abbey Churchyard, Bath, United Kingdom.

Features: These guided walking tours offer an excellent way to explore Bath's rich history and stunning architecture. Led by knowledgeable guides, tourists can discover hidden gems and iconic landmarks of the city.

Herschel Museum of Astronomy

Address: 19 New King St, Bath BA1 2BL, United Kingdom.

Features: This museum is dedicated to the astronomer William Herschel and his sister Caroline. It is located in their former home and showcases historical telescopes, artifacts, and the story of their contributions to astronomy.

Moorlands Park

Address: Englishcombe Ln, Bath BA2 2DZ, United Kingdom.

Features: Moorlands Park is a peaceful green space ideal for relaxation and leisure activities. It includes a children's play area, making it a family-friendly spot.

No. 1 Royal Crescent

Address: 1 Royal Cres, Bath BA1 2LR, United Kingdom.

Features: This museum is a beautifully restored 18th-century townhouse that forms part of the iconic Royal Crescent. It provides a glimpse into the life of the Georgian era with authentic room displays and furniture.

Beazer Garden Maze

Address: Spring Gardens Rd, Bath, United Kingdom.

Features: This unique garden maze offers a fun and interactive experience. It's a delightful spot for both children and adults to explore.

Museum of Bath Stone

Address: 54A Combe Rd, Bath BA2 5HY, United Kingdom.

Features: This museum is dedicated to the history and use of Bath Stone, a famous local limestone used in the city's architecture. It provides insights into quarrying and the stone's significance in Bath's development.

Museum of Bath Architecture

Address: The Countess of Huntingdon's Chapel, The Paragon, Bath BA1 5NA, United Kingdom.

Features: This museum showcases the architectural history of Bath, highlighting the design and construction of its famous Georgian buildings.

Bath Quays Waterside

Features: Bath Quays Waterside is a modern development along the River Avon, offering scenic walks, dining, and shopping experiences. It's a vibrant addition to Bath's cityscape.

STAYING IN SOMERSET

The Gainsborough Bath Spa

Address: Beau Street, Bath, Somerset BA1 1QY, UK

Offerings: Luxury spa hotel offering exclusive access to natural thermal waters. Features elegantly designed rooms, a spa, and an upscale restaurant.

Estimated Cost: Approximately £250 - £500 per night

Website:
https://www.thegainsboroughbathspa.co.uk/

Babington House

Address: Babington House, Babington, Nr Frome, Somerset BA11 3RW, UK

Offerings: A stylish, countryside hotel set in a Georgian manor offering comfortable rooms, a spa, and fine dining. Known for its picturesque surroundings and exclusive atmosphere.

Estimated Cost: Around £300 - £600 per night

Website: https://www.babingtonhouse.co.uk/

The Bath Priory

Address: Weston Road, Bath, Somerset BA1 2XT, UK

Offerings: A luxurious hotel in a historic house featuring a garden, an acclaimed restaurant, and a spa. Offers a blend of traditional elegance and modern comfort.

Estimated Cost: Approximately £200 - £400 per night

Website: https://www.thebathpriory.co.uk/

The Royal Crescent Hotel & Spa

Address: 16 Royal Crescent, Bath, Somerset BA1 2LS, UK

Offerings: Set in the iconic Royal Crescent, this hotel offers luxurious rooms, a full-service spa, and a fine dining restaurant. Ideal for experiencing historic Bath in style.

Estimated Cost: About £350 - £700 per night

Website: https://www.royalcrescent.co.uk/

Bannatyne Hotel- Charlton House

Address: Charlton Rd, Shepton Mallet, Somerset BA4 4PR, UK

Offerings: A spa hotel offering a blend of luxury and wellness. Features elegant rooms, a restaurant, and extensive spa facilities.

Estimated Cost: Around £150 - £300 per night

Ston Easton Park

Address: Ston Easton, Somerset BA3 4DF, UK

Offerings: A grand Palladian mansion set in vast parklands, offering luxurious rooms, fine dining, and stunning gardens.

Estimated Cost: Approximately £200 - £400 per night

Website: https://www.stoneaston.co.uk/

The Castle at Taunton

Address: Castle Green, Taunton, Somerset TA1 1NF, UK

Offerings: Historic hotel in the heart of Taunton with comfortable rooms, a renowned restaurant, and charming gardens.

Estimated Cost: About £100 - £250 per night

Website: https://www.the-castle-hotel.com/

Homewood Hotel & Spa

Address: Abbey Ln, Freshford, Bath, Somerset BA2 7TB, UK
Offerings: Boutique country house hotel with a spa, fine dining, and uniquely decorated rooms. Offers a blend of contemporary style and classic charm.
Estimated Cost: Approximately £150 - £350 per night
Website: https://www.homewoodbath.co.uk/

AFFORDABLE ACCOMMODATION OPTIONS IN SOMERSET:

Premier Inn Taunton East

Address: 81 Bridgwater Rd, Taunton, Somerset TA1 2DU, UK
Offerings: Known for providing comfortable rooms at an affordable price. Includes free Wi-Fi, a restaurant, and family rooms.
Estimated Cost: Around £50 - £100 per night

Travelodge Bath Waterside

Address: Rossiter Rd, Widcombe Basin, Bath BA2 4JP, UK
Offerings: Budget-friendly hotel close to the city center, offering basic but comfortable rooms. Ideal for travelers looking to explore Bath.
Estimated Cost: Approximately £40 - £90 per night

The Bear Inn by Marston's Inns

Address: 53 High St, Street, Somerset BA16 0EF, UK
Offerings: A traditional inn offering cozy rooms, a pub, and dining facilities. Good for a comfortable stay without breaking the bank.
Estimated Cost: Around £60 - £120 per night

Holiday Inn Express Taunton

Address: Blackbrook Park Ave, Taunton, Somerset TA1 2PX, UK
Offerings: Offers modern rooms with free breakfast and Wi-Fi. Suitable for both business and leisure travelers.
Estimated Cost: About £60 - £110 per night

Bath YMCA

Address: International House, Broad St Pl, Bath BA1 5LH, UK
Offerings: A budget-friendly option in the heart of Bath, offering dormitory-style rooms and private rooms.
Estimated Cost: Approximately £25 - £70 per night
Website: https://www.bathymca.co.uk/

Days Inn by Wyndham Taunton

Address: Taunton Deane Service Area, Trull, Taunton, Somerset TA3 7PF, UK
Offerings: Provides affordable accommodation with easy access to the M5 motorway. Pet-friendly with free parking.
Estimated Cost: Around £40 - £80 per night

Ibis Bridgwater

Address: Woodlands Ct Business Park, Bristol Rd, Bridgwater TA6 4FJ, UK
Offerings: Modern and affordable, offering comfortable rooms, a restaurant, and bar.
Estimated Cost: About £45 - £90 per night

Z Hotel Bath

Address: 7 Saw Cl, Bath BA1 1EY, UK
Offerings: Situated in the city center, known for compact and stylishly designed rooms. Great for budget-conscious travelers.
Estimated Cost: Approximately £50 - £100 per night

STAYING IN BATHS

Luxury Options

The Royal Crescent Hotel & Spa
Address: 16 Royal Crescent, Bath BA1 2LS, UK
Features: Iconic location, luxury spa, elegant rooms, and fine dining.
Estimated Cost: Starting from around £250 per night.
Website: https://www.royalcrescent.co.uk/

The Gainsborough Bath Spa
Address: Beau Street, Bath BA1 1QY, UK
Features: 5-star hotel, exclusive access to natural thermal waters, luxurious spa treatments.
Estimated Cost: From £300 per night.
Website: https://www.thegainsboroughbathspa.co.uk/

The Bath Priory
Address: Weston Road, Bath BA1 2XT, UK
Features: Historic building, beautiful gardens, gourmet restaurant, and a relaxing spa.
Estimated Cost: Around £200-£400 per night.
Website: https://www.thebathpriory.co.uk/

Affordable Options

Z Hotel Bath
Address: 7 Saw Cl, Bath BA1 1EY, UK
Features: Contemporary design, central location, affordable luxury.
Estimated Cost: From £50 per night.
Website: Z Hotel Bath

Holiday Inn Express Bath
Address: Lower Bristol Rd, Brougham Hayes, Bath BA2 3QU, UK
Features: Modern and comfortable, includes breakfast, close to city center.
Estimated Cost: Starting from £70 per night.

Premier Inn Bath City Centre Hotel
Address: James St W, Bath BA1 2BX, UK
Features: Affordable, comfortable, centrally located.
Estimated Cost: Around £60-£100 per night.
Website: Premier Inn Bath

Boutique Options

Henrietta House
Address: 27-29 Henrietta St, Bath BA2 6LR, UK
Features: Georgian townhouse, charming decor, breakfast included.
Estimated Cost: From £120 per night.
Website: https://www.henriettahouse.co.uk/

No.15 Great Pulteney
Address: 15 Great Pulteney St, Bath BA2 4BR, UK
Features: Unique boutique hotel, spa, and artfully designed rooms.
Estimated Cost: £150-£250 per night.
Website: https://no15greatpulteney.co.uk/

DINING IN SOMERSET: WHERE TO EAT

The Pony & Trap

Address: Moorledge Rd, Chew Magna, Bristol BS40 8TQ, UK
Type of Meals: Gastro-pub fare, locally sourced ingredients.
Estimated Cost: ££ - £££
Website: https://www.theponyandtrap.co.uk/

The Ethicurean

Address: Barley Wood Walled Garden, Long Ln, Wrington, Bristol BS40 5SA, UK
Type of Meals: Seasonal British cuisine, ethically sourced ingredients.
Estimated Cost: ££ - £££
Website: https://www.theethicurean.com/

The Scallop Shell

Address: 22 Monmouth Pl, Bath BA1 2AY, UK
Type of Meals: Seafood, particularly known for fish and chips.
Estimated Cost: ££
Website: https://thescallopshell.co.uk/

Woods Restaurant

Address: 9-13 Alfred St, Bath BA1 2QX, UK
Type of Meals: Modern British cuisine.
Estimated Cost: ££ - £££
Website: http://www.woodsrestaurant.com/

Clavelshay Barn

Address: Lower Clavelshay Farm, North Petherton, Bridgwater TA6 6PJ, UK
Type of Meals: Farm-to-table dining experience.
Estimated Cost: £££
Website: https://www.clavelshaybarn.co.uk/

Duende

Address: 3A Luttrell House, 13 High St, Wiveliscombe, Taunton TA4 2JX, UK
Type of Meals: Fine dining, inventive dishes.
Estimated Cost: £££
Website: https://www.duenderestaurant.co.uk/

Castle Bow Restaurant

Address: Castle Green, Taunton TA1 1NF, UK
Type of Meals: Contemporary British, fine dining.
Estimated Cost: ££££
Website: https://www.castlebow.com/

Bocabar

Address: Red Brick Building, Morland Rd, Glastonbury BA6 9FT, UK
Type of Meals: Eclectic menu, pizzas, and local ales.
Estimated Cost: ££
Website: https://www.bocabar.co.uk/

Matt's Kitchen

Address: 51 High St, Bruton BA10 0AW, UK
Type of Meals: Home-cooked style meals in a cozy setting.
Estimated Cost: ££
Website: http://www.mattskitchen.co.uk/

Roth Bar & Grill

Address: Durslade Farm, Dropping Ln, Bruton BA10 0NL, UK
Type of Meals: Grill, modern British.
Estimated Cost: ££ - £££
Website: https://www.rothbarandgrill.co.uk/

DINING IN BATHS: WHERE TO EAT

Sotto Sotto

Address: 10 North Parade, Bath BA2 4AL, UK
Type of Meals: Authentic Italian cuisine
Website: http://www.sottosotto.co.uk/

The Ivy Bath Brasserie

Address: 39 Milsom St, Bath BA1 1DS, UK
Type of Meals: Modern British & international classics
Website: https://theivybathbrasserie.com/

The Scallop Shell

Address: 22 Monmouth Pl, Bath BA1 2AY, UK
Type of Meals: Seafood, particularly known for fish and chips
Website: https://thescallopshell.co.uk/

Acorn Restaurant

Address: 2 North Parade Passage, Bath BA1 1NX, UK
Type of Meals: Plant-based, vegan, and vegetarian dishes
Website: https://www.acornrestaurant.co.uk/

Green Park Brasserie

Address: Green Park Station, Bath BA1 1JB, UK
Type of Meals: Modern British with live jazz music
Website:
https://www.greenparkbrasserie.com/

OAK Restaurant

Address: 1 Green St, Bath BA1 2JZ, UK
Type of Meals: Organic, seasonal ingredients in a stylish setting
Website: https://www.oakrestaurant.co.uk/

Clayton's Kitchen

Address: 15A George St, Bath BA1 2EN, UK
Type of Meals: Modern European cuisine
Estimated Cost: ££ - £££
Website: https://www.claytonskitchen.com/

Menu Gordon Jones

Address: 2 Wellsway, Bath BA2 3AQ, UK
Type of Meals: Innovative tasting menus
Website:
http://www.menugordonjones.co.uk/

Yak Yeti Yak

Address: 12 Pierrepont St, Bath BA1 1LA, UK
Type of Meals: Nepalese cuisine
Website: http://www.yakyetiyak.co.uk/

Same-Same but Different

Address: 7A Princes Buildings, George St, Bath BA1 2ED, UK
Type of Meals: European and Mediterranean
Website: https://www.same-same.co.uk/

Sally Lunn's Historic Eating House & Museum

Address: 4 North Parade Passage, Bath BA1 1NX, UK
Type of Meals: Home of the famous Sally Lunn Bun
Website: https://www.sallylunns.co.uk/

CULTURAL INSIGHTS

Somerset's Cultural Insights

Historical Significance: Somerset is steeped in history, from the ancient Roman Baths in Bath to the medieval Glastonbury Abbey, believed to be the burial site of King Arthur. Its landscape is dotted with historical landmarks like the mystical Chalice Well and the imposing Dunster Castle.

Folklore and Legends: The county is a hotspot for folklore, including the tales of King Arthur and the Holy Grail. Glastonbury Tor is often associated with the mythical Isle of Avalon.

Agriculture and Cider Making: Somerset's rural landscape is deeply connected to agriculture, especially known for its cider production. The area boasts numerous cider farms where traditional methods are still used.

Arts and Music: Somerset hosts the world-famous Glastonbury Festival, attracting global music and arts enthusiasts. The area's creative spirit is also reflected in its numerous art galleries and artisan workshops.

Architecture: From the Georgian elegance of Bath to the rustic charm of Somerset's village cottages, the region showcases a diverse architectural heritage.

Bath's Cultural Insights

Roman and Georgian Influence: Bath is renowned for its Roman Baths and stunning Georgian architecture, evident in landmarks like the Royal Crescent and the Circus.

Literary Connections: Bath has strong ties to literature, notably Jane Austen, who lived here and set two of her novels in the city.

Thermal Spa City: The city's natural hot springs have been a draw for centuries, culminating in modern-day spas like Thermae Bath Spa where visitors can enjoy the mineral-rich waters.

Cultural Festivals: Bath hosts numerous cultural events, including the Bath Literature Festival, Bath Film Festival, and Bath Mozartfest, reflecting its vibrant cultural scene.

Art and Museums: With numerous galleries and museums like The Holburne Museum and Victoria Art Gallery, Bath offers a rich art scene. The Fashion Museum showcases fashion from the 1600s to the present day.

Culinary Scene: Bath's culinary offerings range from traditional tea houses like Sally Lunn's to contemporary fine dining establishments, reflecting a blend of historic and modern tastes.

Performing Arts: The city has a lively performing arts scene, anchored by the Theatre Royal, one of the oldest and most respected theatres in the UK.

CUSTOM ITINERARIES FOR SOMERSET

Historical and Cultural Explorer (3-4 Days)

Day 1: Bath

Morning: Visit the Roman Baths and Bath Abbey.

Afternoon: Explore the Royal Crescent and the Circus, followed by a visit to the Jane Austen Centre.

Evening: Dine in one of Bath's historic restaurants or pubs.

Day 2: Glastonbury and Wells

Morning: Tour Glastonbury Abbey and climb the Tor.

Afternoon: Head to Wells, visit Wells Cathedral and Bishop's Palace.

Evening: Enjoy a meal in Wells.

Day 3: Historic Houses and Gardens

Visit Montacute House and Lytes Cary Manor. Explore the gardens and enjoy a traditional English tea.

Day 4: Museums and Art

Visit the Somerset Rural Life Museum and the Museum of Somerset.

Spend the afternoon in a local art gallery or craft workshop.

Nature and Outdoor Adventure (2-3 Days)

Day 1: Hiking and Exploring

Spend the day hiking in the Mendip Hills, exploring Cheddar Gorge and Ebbor Gorge.

Evening at a countryside pub.

Day 2: Coastal Somerset

Visit Burnham-on-Sea beach and Brean Down Fort.

Enjoy seaside activities and a beachside dinner.

Day 3: Country Parks and Gardens

Explore Hestercombe Gardens and Vivary Park.

Optional visit to Ham Hill Country Park for sunset views.

Family-Friendly Fun (2-3 Days)

Day 1: Family Attractions

Visit the Wookey Hole Caves and the Cheddar Gorge & Caves.

Evening: Dinner at a family-friendly restaurant in Cheddar.

Day 2: Animal Adventures and Theme Parks

Spend the day at the Animal Farm Adventure Park.

Visit Brean Theme Park in the afternoon.

Day 3: Educational and Interactive

Explore the Museum of Somerset.

Visit the Somerset Space Walk or RSPB Ham Wall for a nature walk.

Relaxation and Wellness (2 Days)

Day 1: Spa and Wellness
Spend the day at Thermae Bath Spa.
Evening: Enjoy a quiet dinner in Bath.

Day 2: Scenic Walks and Quiet Exploration
Morning at the National Trust - Prior Park Landscape Garden.
Afternoon: Gentle walks in the countryside, like the Bath Skyline Walk.

Food and Cider Enthusiast (2 Days)

Day 1: Culinary Exploration in Bath
Explore Bath's culinary scene, with a focus on local and seasonal produce.
Visit local markets and specialty food shops.

Day 2: Cider and Cheese Tour
Tour a local cider farm in Somerset.
Visit Cheddar to sample Cheddar cheese and explore the village.

HISTORICAL SNAPSHOT: SOMERSET'S LEGACY

Prehistoric Beginnings

Ancient Monuments and Early Inhabitants: Somerset's landscape is dotted with enigmatic relics from prehistoric times. The ceremonial sites at Stanton Drew are among the most intriguing, featuring one of the largest stone circles in Britain. These ancient structures evoke a sense of mystery, suggesting that early communities gathered here for significant rituals and social events. Similarly, the Neolithic causewayed enclosure at Windmill Hill hints at early agricultural practices and social structures, providing valuable insights into the lives of Somerset's earliest inhabitants.

Glastonbury Tor: Rising majestically from the Somerset Levels, Glastonbury Tor is a place shrouded in myths and legends. This conical hill, topped by the remains of St. Michael's Tower, has been revered since ancient times. It's a site deeply entwined with the Arthurian legends, often associated with Avalon, a mythical island from the King Arthur tales. The Tor is also linked to the Holy Grail, the legendary cup from Christian mythology. Pilgrims and visitors are drawn to this mystical spot, not only for its historical significance but also for its spiritual ambiance and panoramic views of the surrounding countryside.

Roman and Saxon Era

Roman Occupation

Foundation of Bath (Aquae Sulis): The Romans established Bath, known then as Aquae Sulis, around the naturally occurring hot springs, a rare phenomenon in Britain. They recognized the springs' potential and constructed elaborate baths, turning the area into a significant religious and healing center. The Roman Baths that we see today are a testament to their engineering prowess and understanding of leisure and hygiene.

Roman Architecture and Culture: Alongside the famous baths, the Romans erected a temple dedicated to Sulis Minerva, amalgamating the local deity Sulis with the Roman goddess Minerva. The presence of these grand structures highlights the importance of Aquae Sulis as a spiritual and cultural hub in Roman Britain. The blend of Roman and native traditions here exemplifies the cultural syncretism that occurred during the Roman occupation.

Saxon Stronghold

Post-Roman Transformation: After the Roman withdrawal from Britain, the region witnessed significant changes. The Saxons stepped into the power vacuum, establishing control over large parts of what is now England. Somerset became a pivotal region in the emerging Kingdom of Wessex.

King Alfred the Great: Born in Somerset, King Alfred the Great is a seminal figure in English history. His reign (871-899 AD) was marked by intellectual revival and military success. Most notably, he was instrumental in defending his realm against Viking invasions, playing a critical role in shaping the early history of England. His strategies in warfare and his efforts in promoting education and legal reform had lasting impacts on English society.

The Medieval Period in Somerset

Monastic Somerset

Glastonbury Abbey: One of the most renowned monastic centers in England, Glastonbury Abbey, played a pivotal role in Somerset's religious and cultural landscape. It was famed for its wealth and influence, attracting pilgrims from far and wide. The Abbey's history is intertwined with Christian legends, including the story that it was founded by Joseph of Arimathea. It was also believed to be the burial site of King Arthur and Queen Guinevere, adding to its mystique and spiritual significance.

Other Monastic Institutions: Beyond Glastonbury, Somerset was home to several other important monasteries and abbeys, such as Muchelney Abbey and Cleeve Abbey. These institutions were not just religious centers but also hubs of education, manuscript production, and charity.

Agricultural Development

Wool Industry: The Middle Ages saw Somerset prospering from the wool trade. The county's sheep farming and wool production became significant economic drivers, leading to wealth accumulation and the growth of market towns. Towns like Frome and Wells owe their development to the wool trade, which facilitated urban growth and architectural advancements.

Market Towns: This era witnessed the rise of market towns, which became centers of commerce and social interaction. These towns were crucial in the local economy, serving as trading hubs for agricultural produce, particularly wool, and craft goods. The marketplaces and town squares that emerged during this period remain central to many of Somerset's towns today.

Tudor Times to the Industrial Revolution in Somerset

Religious and Civil Strife

Dissolution of the Monasteries: Under King Henry VIII, the Dissolution of the Monasteries (1536–1541) profoundly affected Somerset. Monastic institutions like Glastonbury Abbey, which had been centers of religious life, education, and economic activity, were dismantled. This not only altered the religious landscape but also had significant economic and social repercussions, as these institutions were major landowners and employers.

Civil War: During the English Civil War (1642–1651), Somerset was a strategically important area and witnessed several key battles and skirmishes. The county's allegiances were divided, with both Royalist and Parliamentarian forces vying for control. Notable events included the Siege of Taunton and the Battle of Langport, which were crucial in the conflict's outcome.

Industrial Growth

Coal Mining: The 18th and 19th centuries heralded the rise of industrial activity in Somerset, particularly coal mining. The Radstock area in the Somerset coalfield became a hub for coal extraction, contributing significantly to the region's economic development. This period saw the growth of mining communities and the transformation of the landscape due to industrial activities.

Somerset Coal Canal: Established in the late 18th century, the Somerset Coal Canal was a crucial infrastructure project that facilitated the transport of coal from mines in the Somerset coalfield to larger markets. This canal played a vital role in the industrialization of the region, improving the efficiency of coal transportation and fueling further industrial growth.

Textile Industry: Alongside mining, Somerset also saw the development of its textile industry during this period. Towns like Frome became known for their woolen and later silk production. This industry played a significant role in the economic landscape of the county, contributing to urban growth and employment.

CUSTOM ITINERARIES FOR BATHS

Historical and Architectural Enthusiast (2 Days)

Day 1: Bath's Historic Core

Morning: Visit the Roman Baths, followed by Bath Abbey.

Afternoon: Explore the Royal Crescent, the Circus, and Pulteney Bridge.

Evening: Dine in a Georgian-era themed restaurant.

Day 2: Art and Culture

Morning: Visit the Holburne Museum and the Jane Austen Centre.

Afternoon: Stroll through the Victoria Art Gallery and Bath's artisan quarter for local crafts.

Evening: Attend a performance at the Theatre Royal or a concert in a historical venue.

Relaxation and Wellness Seeker (1-2 Days)

Day 1: Spa Day

Spend the day at Thermae Bath Spa, enjoying the rooftop pool and various treatments.

Evening: Relaxing dinner at a quiet, cozy restaurant.

Day 2: Nature and Serenity

Morning: Visit the National Trust - Prior Park Landscape Garden.

Afternoon: Gentle walks in the Sydney Gardens or along the Avon River.

Evening: Casual dining in a riverside café.

Family-Friendly Discovery (2 Days)

Day 1: Educational Fun

Visit the Roman Baths and participate in family-friendly activities.

Afternoon at the Bath Sports and Leisure Centre for indoor swimming and games.

Evening: Dinner at a family-friendly restaurant.

Day 2: Interactive Learning

Morning at the Herschel Museum of Astronomy.

Afternoon: Explore the Bath City Farm or the Bath Ghost Tours for older kids.

Evening: Casual dinner and a stroll through the city centre.

Art and Literature Lover (2 Days)

Day 1: Literary Bath

Morning: The Jane Austen Centre, followed by a visit to Mr. B's Emporium of Reading Delights (bookshop).

Afternoon: Visit the Bath Central Library or a literary-themed café.

Evening: Attend a reading or a literary event (check local listings).

Day 2: Artistic Pursuits

Morning: Holburne Museum and Victoria Art Gallery.

Afternoon: Join an art workshop or visit local galleries.

Evening: Dine in an art café or restaurant with local art on display.

Culinary Explorer (1-2 Days)

Day 1: Gastronomic Tour

Morning: Visit local markets (like Green Park Station market).

Afternoon: Join a food tour or visit artisanal food shops.

Evening: Dinner at a restaurant known for contemporary British cuisine.

Day 2: Tea and Treats

Morning: Breakfast in a historic café (like Sally Lunn's).

Afternoon: Attend a high tea experience.

Evening: Explore craft pubs and bars, sampling local ciders and ales.

FUN FACTS ABOUT BATHS

Bath, a city known for its Roman-built baths and Georgian architecture, holds many interesting facts. Here's a fun and lesser-known fact about Bath:

Thermal Springs: The Only Hot Springs in the UK

Natural Phenomenon: Bath is home to the only natural hot springs in the United Kingdom. These springs are the reason the Romans founded the city around 60 AD, calling it Aquae Sulis.

Unique Composition: The water in these springs contains 43 different minerals, making it unique. It's been said that this mineral-rich water has healing properties.

Flow Rate and Temperature: The three hot springs in Bath - the King's Spring, the Hetling Spring, and the Cross Bath Spring - deliver over a million liters of hot water every day at a temperature of about 45°C (113°F).

Historical Significance: The Roman Baths around these springs are remarkably well-preserved and have been a destination for relaxation and health for over 2,000 years.

PART 4: SOUTH WEST CORNWALL – JOURNEY THROUGH A COASTAL PARADISE

WELCOMING TO CORNWALL

Located in the southwestern tip of England, Cornwall beckons with its rugged coastline, enchanting landscapes, and a rich history and culture. This picturesque county, surrounded by the Atlantic Ocean and the English Channel, offers a unique blend of captivating scenery, artistic heritage, and a warm, welcoming atmosphere. Here's an introduction to the wonders of Cornwall:

Majestic Coastline and Beaches

Stunning Seascapes: Cornwall's coastline is a breathtaking spectacle of dramatic cliffs, golden sandy beaches, and hidden coves. It's a paradise for surfers, swimmers, and sun-seekers, with famous beaches like Fistral and Porthmeor drawing visitors from all over.

Cornish Riviera: The south coast of Cornwall, often referred to as the Cornish Riviera, is known for its gentler landscape, with picturesque harbors such as Fowey and St Mawes, and idyllic beaches like Polkerris and Pentewan.

Rich Cultural Heritage

Cornish Language and Traditions: Cornwall has its own distinct identity, with a strong sense of tradition and culture. The Cornish language, though less commonly spoken now, is experiencing a revival. Annual cultural events, like St Piran's Day, celebrate Cornwall's heritage and community spirit.

Artistic Hub: Artists have long been drawn to Cornwall's unique light and scenic beauty. St Ives, in particular, is famed for its artist community and the Tate St Ives gallery. The county's artistic legacy continues to thrive, with numerous galleries and craft centers showcasing local talent.

Historical Landmarks

Cornish Mining Heritage: The landscape is dotted with remnants of its mining past, part of the Cornwall and West Devon Mining Landscape UNESCO World Heritage Site. The dramatic ruins of engine houses and mines stand as a testament to Cornwall's industrial heritage.

Ancient Sites: Cornwall is also home to a wealth of ancient monuments and sites, including the mystical Tintagel Castle, believed to be linked to the legend of King Arthur, and the prehistoric stone circles of Bodmin Moor.

Culinary Delights

Cornish Cuisine: Cornwall's culinary scene is a delight, especially known for its seafood and traditional dishes like Cornish pasties. Local produce, from clotted cream to Cornish cheeses, plays a vital role in the county's gastronomic offerings.

Food Festivals: Food festivals celebrate Cornwall's culinary heritage, with events like the Falmouth Oyster Festival and the Great Cornish Food Festival drawing food enthusiasts.

Natural Wonders

Gardens and Nature Reserves: The county's mild climate allows for some of the most beautiful gardens in the UK, such as the Lost Gardens of Heligan and the Eden Project. Nature reserves offer serene escapes and opportunities to observe Cornwall's diverse wildlife.

Active and Leisure Activities

Outdoor Adventures: Cornwall's varied landscape is perfect for outdoor activities. Hiking the South West Coast Path, surfing in Newquay, or sailing in the Fal Estuary – there's something for every adventurer.

Relaxation and Wellness: For those seeking relaxation, Cornwall's serene environment and wellness retreats offer a perfect escape to unwind and rejuvenate.

ATTRACTIONS IN CORNWALL

The Lost Gardens of Heligan

Address: B3273, Pentewan, Saint Austell PL26 6EN, United Kingdom

Description: Once lost under overgrowth for decades, The Lost Gardens of Heligan have been beautifully restored to their former glory. This 200-acre site offers a diverse range of gardens, from Victorian Productive Gardens to lush sub-tropical jungles.

Highlights: Explore the Italian Garden, the Melon Yard, and the remarkable "Mud Maid" sculpture. The estate also features ancient woodlands and a series of lakes fed by a ram pump over a century old.

Opening Hours: Typically open from 10 AM to 5 PM, with last entry at 4 PM.

Website: https://www.heligan.com/

Estimated Cost: Adult tickets are around £15, with concessions available for seniors and students. Children's tickets (aged 5-17) are priced lower, and there are family ticket options.

Land's End

Address: Land's End, Sennen, Penzance TR19 7AA, United Kingdom

Description: Land's End is one of Britain's most famous landmarks, known fo r its unique location at the tip of Cornwall. It offers stunning views over the Atlantic Ocean and features a range of family-friendly attractions, shops, and eateries.

Highlights: Attractions include the 4D film experience, the Shaun the Sheep Experience, and various exhibitions. The landmark signpost is a popular spot for photos.

Opening Hours: The site is generally open from 10 AM, but closing times can vary seasonally.

Website: https://www.landsend-landmark.co.uk/

Estimated Cost: Entry to the site is free, but parking charges apply. Additional costs for attractions vary.

Lappa Valley

Address: St Newlyn East, Newquay TR8 5LX, United Kingdom

Description: Lappa Valley is a delightful attraction for families, particularly those with young children. It features miniature steam trains that take visitors on a journey through a scenic conservation area.

Highlights: Besides the steam railway, there are canoeing activities, a maze, mini-golf, and play areas.

Opening Hours: Opens at 9:30 AM, with last admission at 4:20 PM.

Website: https://www.lappavalley.co.uk/

Estimated Cost: Prices for adults and children are around £12.95, with children under 3 free. Family tickets are also available.

Newquay Zoo

Address: Trenance Gardens, Newquay TR7 2LZ, United Kingdom

Description: Newquay Zoo is a vibrant and educational zoo, home to hundreds of unique and endangered animals. It's set within lush tropical gardens just a short distance from Newquay's center.

Highlights: The zoo showcases a range of animals from around the world, offering animal experiences and educational talks.

Opening Hours: Generally open from 10 AM to 4:30 PM.

Website: https://www.newquayzoo.org.uk/

Estimated Cost: Adult tickets are approximately £15.25, while children's tickets (3-15 years) are around £11.50. There are family tickets and group discounts available.

National Trust- Carnewas at Bedruthan

Address: Carnewas at Bedruthan, Mawgan Porth, near Newquay, Cornwall, TR8 4BQ, UK

Description: Carnewas at Bedruthan is a spectacular stretch of coastline offering dramatic views, stunning clifftop walks, and fascinating geological formations.

Highlights: The clifftop paths provide excellent vantage points for photography and birdwatching, with a backdrop of dramatic cliffs and sea stacks.

Opening Hours: Open daily until 5 PM.

Estimated Cost: Free access to the outdoor areas; parking fees apply for non-National Trust members.

Pendennis Castle

Address: Castle Drive, Falmouth, Cornwall, TR11 4LP, UK

Description: Pendennis Castle is a formidable fortress built by Henry VIII. The castle has defended Cornwall against foreign invasion since the Tudor times and offers a glimpse into Cornwall's military history.

Highlights: The castle features interactive exhibits, artillery displays, and offers panoramic views of the Cornish coastline.

Opening Hours: Open from 10 AM to 4 PM. It's advisable to check their website for seasonal variations.

Estimated Cost: Adult tickets are around £12.60, with concessions and family tickets available.

Merlin's Cave

Address: Atlantic Road, Tintagel, Cornwall, PL34 0DB, UK

Description: Merlin's Cave is a mythical sea cave located beneath Tintagel Castle, associated with the legendary wizard Merlin. The cave is accessible at low tide.

Highlights: The cave offers an atmospheric setting, with its connection to Arthurian legends adding to its appeal. It's a popular spot for photography and exploration.

Opening Hours: Open 24 hours, but access is dependent on tide times.

Estimated Cost: Free to visit, but caution is advised during tidal changes.

National Trust- Trelissick Garden

Address: Feock, near Truro, Cornwall, TR3 6QL, UK

Description: Trelissick Garden, perched at the head of the Fal Estuary, boasts stunning garden walks, varied plant species, and impressive river views.

Highlights: The garden offers a diverse range of flora, year-round color, and scenic riverside walks. There's also a gallery and cafe on-site.

Opening Hours: Open until 4:30 PM, but the timing can vary, so it's best to check the website before visiting.

Estimated Cost: Entry is free for National Trust members. Non-member adult tickets are approximately £12.60.

National Maritime Museum Cornwall

Address: Discovery Quay, Falmouth, Cornwall, TR11 3QY, UK

Description: This museum celebrates Cornwall's rich maritime history through interactive exhibits and extensive collections. It offers a deep dive into the region's relationship with the sea.

Highlights: Features include exhibitions on local seafaring heritage, boat collections, and maritime art. The museum also hosts special events and activities suitable for all ages.

Opening Hours: Open until 5 PM. It's best to check the website for specific timing details, especially for special exhibitions.

Website: https://nmmc.co.uk/

Estimated Cost: Adult tickets are approximately £13.95, with discounts for children, families, and seniors.

Roche Rock

Address: Near Cricket Club, Roche, Cornwall, UK

Description: Roche Rock is a unique geological formation and a site of historical significance. It's renowned for its rugged beauty and the ruins of a medieval hermitage perched atop the rock.

Highlights: Ideal for explorers and history enthusiasts, it offers a chance to see a part of Cornwall's lesser-known heritage. The site is also a popular spot for photography.

Opening Hours: Open 24 hours, but accessibility may depend on weather conditions.

Estimated Cost: Free to visit.

Trebah Garden

Address: Mawnan Smith, near Falmouth, Cornwall, TR11 5JZ, UK

Description: Trebah is a beautiful subtropical garden leading down to a private beach on the Helford River. It's known for its vibrant plants and tranquil atmosphere.

Highlights: The garden features a collection of rare and exotic plants, with scenic paths winding down to a secluded beach. It's a perfect spot for nature lovers and families.

Opening Hours: Open until 4:30 PM. Please verify the current opening times on their website.

Website: https://www.trebahgarden.co.uk/

Estimated Cost: Adult entry is around £12, with concessions for children and families.

Polperro Model Village

Address: Mill Hill, Polperro, Cornwall, PL13 2RP, UK

Description: This charming model village is a miniature representation of Polperro, complete with a model railway and detailed landscaping.

Highlights: It's a delightful attraction for families, offering a whimsical view of Cornish village life in miniature. The model railway is a particular highlight.

Opening Hours: Open until 5:30 PM. Check their website or local tourist information for seasonal variations.

Estimated Cost: Entry fees are modest, usually around a few pounds per person.

National Trust- Trerice

Address: Kestle Mill, near Newquay, Cornwall, TR8 4PG, UK

Description: Trerice is a charming Elizabethan manor house with fine interiors and a peaceful garden.

Highlights: The property is known for its exquisite Elizabethan architecture and beautiful garden. It's a great place for history buffs and those looking for a tranquil setting.

Opening Hours: Currently closed. It's recommended to check their website for reopening dates and times.

Estimated Cost: Admission fees apply for non-National Trust members. Typically, adult tickets are around £10-£12.

Golitha Falls

Address: Near Liskeard, Cornwall, UK

Description: Golitha Falls is a series of cascading waterfalls in a picturesque wooded valley on the River Fowey.

Highlights: The falls are set within an area of outstanding natural beauty, perfect for nature lovers and photographers. The site offers several walking trails through ancient woodlands.

Opening Hours: Open 24 hours, but best visited during daylight for safety.

Estimated Cost: Free to visit.

St Mawes Castle

Address: Castle Drive, St Mawes, Cornwall, TR2 5DE, UK

Description: St Mawes Castle is a well-preserved coastal fortress built by Henry VIII, offering stunning views over the sea.

Highlights: Visitors can explore the castle's grounds and interiors, including its gun platform and picturesque gardens.

Opening Hours: Closing soon at 4 PM. Visit their website for the latest opening times.

Estimated Cost: Adult tickets are approximately £10, with concessions for children and families.

Tintagel Castle

Address: Castle Road, Tintagel, Cornwall, PL34 0HE, UK

Description: A medieval fortification associated with the legends of King Arthur, offering dramatic coastal views.

Highlights: The castle ruins are a blend of history and legend, perched on rugged cliffs above the Atlantic. The recently installed bridge offers easy access to the island.

Opening Hours: Closing soon at 4 PM. Check the website for current timings.

Estimated Cost: Adult entry is around £14.50, with discounts available.

Paradise Park and JungleBarn Cornwall

Address: 16 Trelissick Rd, Hayle, Cornwall, TR27 4HB, UK

Description: This attraction combines a wildlife sanctuary with a fun indoor play area.

Highlights: Features a diverse range of birds and animals, educational talks, and a jungle-themed indoor play area for children.

Opening Hours: Closing soon at 4 PM. It's advisable to check for seasonal variations.

Website: https://paradisepark.org.uk/

Estimated Cost: Adult tickets are around £15.95, with family tickets available.

National Trust- Lizard Point

Address: Near Helston, Cornwall, TR12 7NU, UK

Description: The most southerly point of the British mainland, known for its dramatic cliffs and ocean views.

Highlights: The area is perfect for coastal walks, wildlife spotting, and enjoying stunning sea views. It's a must-visit for nature enthusiasts.

Opening Hours: Open 24 hours, but best experienced in daylight.

Estimated Cost: Free to visit, but parking charges may apply for non-National Trust members.

The Minack Theatre

Address: Porthcurno, Penzance, Cornwall, TR19 6JU, UK

Description: This unique open-air amphitheatre is set on the cliffs above the Atlantic Ocean.

Highlights: Famous for its dramatic location and summer season of plays and musicals. It offers breathtaking sea views and a chance to explore the gardens.

Opening Hours: Opening times vary based on events. Check the website for performance schedules.

Website: https://www.minack.com/

Estimated Cost: Ticket prices vary depending on the event.

St Michael's Mount (Harbour View)

Address: Marazion, Cornwall, TR17 0HS, UK

Description: A tidal island crowned by medieval church and castle.

Highlights: Accessible by causeway at low tide or by boat. The island offers a glimpse into a bygone era with its medieval castle and stunning gardens.

Opening Hours: Open until 5 PM. Visit times can depend on the tide.

Website: https://www.stmichaelsmount.co.uk/

Estimated Cost: Entry is around £10 for adults, with concessions available.

Headland

Description: A scenic tourist spot known for its coastal beauty.
Highlights: Ideal for walking, photography, and enjoying panoramic views of the sea.
Opening Hours: Open 24 hours.
Website: Information may be available on local tourism websites.
Estimated Cost: Free to visit.

Pedn Vounder Beach (S W Coast Path)

Description: A picturesque sandy cove beneath craggy cliffs.
Highlights: Known for its clear waters and dramatic landscape. Great for sunbathing, swimming, and coastal walks.
Opening Hours: Open 24 hours, but best visited in daylight.
Estimated Cost: Free access.

National Trust- Cotehele

Address: St Dominick, near Saltash, Cornwall, PL12 6TA, UK
Description: A Tudor house with gardens and an old mill.
Highlights: The estate features a historically significant house, beautiful gardens, and a working watermill.
Opening Hours: Closes soon at 4 PM. Check their website for accurate timings.
Estimated Cost: Admission prices are approximately £12 for adults.

Vale of Avalon / Arthurian Centre (Slaughter Bridge)

Address: Slaughter Bridge, Camelford, Cornwall, PL32 9TT, UK
Description: A site linked to Arthurian legends.
Highlights: Offers a tranquil nature trail and the chance to learn about King Arthur's story.
Opening Hours: Open until 5 PM.
Website: https://www.arthuriancentre.com/
Estimated Cost: Adult tickets are around £6.

Adrenalin Quarry (Lower Clicker Rd)

Address: Lower Clicker Rd, Menheniot, Liskeard, Cornwall, PL14 3PJ, UK
Description: An adventure park offering thrilling activities.
Highlights: Known for its zip wire, giant swing, and coasteering experiences.
Opening Hours: Closing soon at 4 PM. Check for seasonal changes in timings.
Website: https://www.adrenalinquarry.co.uk/
Estimated Cost: Prices vary by activity, with zip wires around £15 per ride.

Carn Euny Ancient Village

Description: An Iron Age settlement with well-preserved remains.
Highlights: Features a fogou (an underground passageway) and informative storyboards.
Opening Hours: Open 24 hours.
Estimated Cost: Free to visit.

Healeys Cornish Cyder Farm

Address: Penhallow, Truro, Cornwall, TR4 9LW, UK
Description: A cider farm offering tours and tastings.
Highlights: Visitors can enjoy guided tours, cider tasting, and explore the farm with its animals.
Opening Hours: Open until 5 PM.
Website: https://healeyscyder.co.uk/
Estimated Cost: Tours are around £15 for adults, with various family packages available.

Historic Port of Charlestown (Charlestown Road)

Address: Charlestown Road, St Austell, Cornwall, PL25 3NJ, UK
Description: A historic Georgian harbor and UNESCO World Heritage Site.
Highlights: Known for its tall ships and as a filming location for several movies and TV shows.
Opening Hours: Open 24 hours.
Estimated Cost: Free to visit, but certain activities or events may have fees.

Polperro Heritage Coast

Description: A charming fishing village known for its idyllic coastal walks and picturesque setting.
Highlights: Explore the narrow streets, enjoy the harbor views, and discover local art galleries.
Opening Hours: Open 24 hours. Best to visit during daylight for the full experience.
Estimated Cost: Free to visit, but some activities in the area may have costs.

St Nectan's Waterfall

Address: Trethevy, Tintagel, Cornwall, PL34 0BG, UK
Description: A tranquil woodland area featuring a stunning waterfall.
Highlights: Ideal for nature lovers and those seeking a peaceful retreat. The waterfall creates a serene atmosphere.
Opening Hours: Opens at 10 AM on Monday.
Website: https://www.stnectansglen.co.uk/
Estimated Cost: Entry fee is around £5.85 for adults.

National Trust- Trengwainton Garden (Boscathnoe Ln)

Address: Madron, Penzance, Cornwall, TR20 8RZ, UK
Description: A historical garden surrounding a 16th-century mansion.
Highlights: Known for its exotic trees, shrubs, and stunning views across Mount's Bay.
Opening Hours: Currently closed. Check the website for updated timings.
Estimated Cost: Entry fees apply for non-National Trust members.

Trethorne Leisure Park

Address: Kennards House, Launceston, Cornwall, PL15 8QE, UK
Description: A family-friendly leisure park offering a variety of activities.
Highlights: Features include bowling, bumper cars, and a petting zoo. Great for a family day out.
Opening Hours: Open until 5 PM.
Website: https://www.trethorneleisure.com/
Estimated Cost: Prices vary depending on activities.

Via Ferrata Cornwall (Via Ferrata Cornwall Goodygrane Activity Centre, Halvasso)

Address: Goodygrane Activity Centre, Halvasso, Cornwall, TR10 9BX, UK
Description: An adventure center offering a unique climbing experience.
Highlights: Features include a via ferrata course, zip wires, and cliff climbing.
Opening Hours: Open until 5 PM.
Website: https://www.viaferratacornwall.co.uk/
Estimated Cost: Activities are priced individually, starting from around £40.

Camel Creek Family Theme Park

Description: A theme park offering rides and attractions for all ages.
Highlights: Temporarily closed, but usually features a range of family-friendly rides and activities.
Website: Check https://www.camelcreek.co.uk/ for updates and reopening information.
Estimated Cost: Ticket prices vary, usually around £15 for adults.

The Viewpoint

Description: An area offering scenic views and a variety of experiences.
Highlights: Ideal for sightseeing, photography, and enjoying the natural beauty of Cornwall.
Opening Hours: Open 24 hours.
Estimated Cost: Free to visit.

Wheal Prosper Tin Mine

Description: An old tin mine offering a glimpse into Cornwall's mining heritage.
Highlights: Visitors can explore the remains of the mine and enjoy coastal walks in the area.
Opening Hours: Open 24 hours.
Estimated Cost: Free to visit.

Castle an Dinas, St Columb Major (UK)

Description: A hillfort with panoramic views and significant historical importance.
Highlights: Known for its breathtaking views and archaeological significance.
Opening Hours: Open 24 hours.
Estimated Cost: Free access.

ACCOMMODATION OPTIONS

Premium Accommodation Options

The Headland Hotel and Spa
Address: Fistral Beach, Newquay, Cornwall, TR7 1EW, UK
Description: A luxurious hotel overlooking Fistral Beach, offering spa facilities, fine dining, and stunning sea views.
Website: https://www.headlandhotel.co.uk/
Estimated Cost: Prices typically start from £240 per night.

The Cornwall Hotel & Spa
Address: Pentewan Road, Tregorrick, St Austell, Cornwall, PL26 7AB, UK
Description: An upscale hotel set in an 1800s manor house, featuring a spa, beautiful grounds, and elegant rooms.
Website: https://www.thecornwall.com/   **Estimated Cost**: Around £152 per night.

Talland Bay Hotel
Address: Porthallow, Looe, Cornwall, PL13 2JB, UK
Description: A stylish hotel with a fine dining restaurant, offering serene ocean views and charming rooms.
Website: https://www.tallandbayhotel.co.uk/
Estimated Cost: Contact hotel for rates.

St Moritz Hotel Cornwall
Address: Trebetherick, Wadebridge, Cornwall, PL27 6SD, UK
Description: A modern, clifftop lodging offering a spa and panoramic sea views, with a contemporary design.
Website: https://www.stmoritzhotel.co.uk/
Estimated Cost: Approximately £250 per night.

Trehellas Country House Hotel, & Restaurant Bodmin /Wadebridge
Address: Washaway, Bodmin, Cornwall, PL30 3AD, UK
Description: A cozy period lodging set in a historic building, featuring a restaurant and a pool.
Estimated Cost: Around £134 per night.

Tregenna Castle Resort
Address: St. Ives, Cornwall, TR26 2DE, UK
Description: A stately hotel with bay views, offering varied dining options and a range of activities.
Website: https://www.tregenna-castle.co.uk/
Estimated Cost: Prices start from £143 per night.

Carbis Bay Hotel & Estate
Address: Carbis Bay, St Ives, Cornwall, TR26 2NP, UK
Description: An upscale beach hotel offering an outdoor pool, spa facilities, and sophisticated dining.
Website: https://www.carbisbayhotel.co.uk/
Estimated Cost: Approximately £458 per night.

The Nare Hotel
Address: Veryan-in-Roseland, Truro, Cornwall, TR2 5PF, UK
Description: A luxurious hotel with plush quarters, dining options, and a spa, set in a picturesque location.
Website: https://www.narehotel.co.uk/
Estimated Cost: Around £1,241 per night.

Mullion Cove Hotel Cornwall
Address: Mullion, Helston, Cornwall, TR12 7EP, UK
Description: An upscale hotel situated in a clifftop setting, offering stunning sea views and refined amenities.
Website: https://www.mullion-cove.co.uk/
Estimated Cost: Starting from £309 per night.

The Carlyon Bay Hotel
Address: Sea Road, Carlyon Bay, St Austell, Cornwall, PL25 3RD, UK
Description: A chic, clifftop hotel featuring sophisticated dining options and panoramic views.
Website: https://www.carlyonbay.com/
Estimated Cost: Prices start at £290 per night.

The Falmouth Hotel
Address: Castle Beach, Falmouth, Cornwall, TR11 4NZ, UK
Description: A Victorian chateau-style hotel located by the sea, offering comfortable rooms with a range of amenities.
Website: https://www.falmouthhotel.co.uk/
Estimated Cost: Prices start from approximately £146 per night.

Best Western Fowey Valley Hotel
Address: Castle Hill, Lostwithiel, Cornwall, PL22 0DD, UK
Description: A bright lodging set in a picturesque location, offering free Wi-Fi and a pool.
Estimated Cost: Around £152 per night.

Wheal Tor Hotel
Address: Caradon Hill, Pensilva, Liskeard, Cornwall, PL14 5PJ, UK
Description: A unique hilltop lodging with dining and bar facilities, offering stunning views of the surrounding area.
Website: https://www.whealtor.co.uk/
Estimated Cost: Approximately £252 per night.

Whipsiderry Hotel, Newquay Cornwall
Address: 12 Watergate Rd, Porth, Newquay, Cornwall, TR7 3LX, UK
Description: A laid-back hotel with a pool and sea views, perfect for a relaxing stay.
Website: https://www.whipsiderry.co.uk/

Fistral Beach Hotel and Spa
Address: Esplanade Rd, Fistral Beach, Newquay, Cornwall, TR7 1PT, UK
Description: A hotel offering bright rooms with sea views, dining, and a spa. Ideal for beach enthusiasts.
Website: https://www.fistralbeachhotel.co.uk/
Estimated Cost: Starting from £206 per night.

The Llawnroc Hotel
Address: Chute Ln, Gorran Haven, Saint Austell, Cornwall, PL26 6NU, UK
Description: An upscale hotel featuring a bar and bistro, located in a charming Cornish village.
Website: https://www.thellawnrochotel.co.uk/

Porth Veor Manor Hotel
Address: Porth Way, Newquay, Cornwall, TR7 3LW, UK
Description: A beach-view hotel offering breakfast and convenient access to the coast.
Website: https://www.porthveormanor.com/

Retallack Resort and Spa Cornwall
Address: Winnards Perch, St Columb Major, Cornwall, TR9 6DE, UK
Description: A lakeside sports resort offering a range of lodges, spa facilities, and activities.
Website: https://www.retallackresort.co.uk/

Camelot Castle Hotel
Address: Camelot Castle, Tintagel, Cornwall, PL34 0DQ, UK
Description: A traditional hotel offering a unique experience with stunning views and a restaurant.
Website: https://www.camelotcastle.com/
Estimated Cost: Approximately £225 per night.

Affordable Accommodation Options

YHA Eden Project
Address: Bodelva, Cornwall, PL24 2SG, UK
Description: An eco-friendly hostel located at the Eden Project, offering unique Sleeper Pods and camping facilities.
Estimated Cost: Pods from £39 per night, with dorm beds and camping options available for less.

Penzance Backpackers
Address: The Blue Dolphin, Alexandra Road, Penzance, Cornwall, TR18 4LZ, UK
Description: A friendly, budget-friendly hostel close to Penzance's town center and seafront.
Estimated Cost: Dorm beds typically from £20-£30 per night.

The Longcross Hotel & Gardens

Address: Trelights, Port Isaac, Cornwall, PL29 3TF, UK

Description: Set in beautiful gardens, this hotel offers a more affordable yet comfortable stay near Port Isaac.

Website: https://www.longcrosshotel.co.uk/

Estimated Cost: Standard rooms around £80-£120 per night.

DINING IN CORNWALL: WHERE TO EAT

Cornwall offers a diverse dining experience, from seafood specialties to cozy cafes and fine dining. Here's a guide to some of the best places to eat:

Seafood Delights

Rick Stein's Seafood Restaurant (Padstow): Renowned chef Rick Stein offers a range of fresh seafood dishes in a sophisticated setting.

The Fish House - Fistral (Newquay): Enjoy fresh, locally-sourced seafood with stunning views of Fistral Beach.

Porthminster Beach Café (St Ives): Offers a unique blend of Mediterranean and Asian seafood cuisine, right on the beach.

Traditional Cornish Fare

The Cornish Arms (St Merryn, Padstow): A traditional pub serving classic Cornish ales and hearty local dishes.

The Gurnard's Head (Zennor): Known for its rustic charm and locally-sourced Cornish ingredients.

St Kew Inn (Bodmin): Offers a delightful traditional Cornish pub experience with a charming garden.

Contemporary and Fine Dining

Paul Ainsworth at No. 6 (Padstow): A Michelin-starred restaurant known for its modern British cuisine.

Oliver's (Falmouth): A cozy, intimate setting offering creative and contemporary dishes.

Kota (Porthleven): Combines local Cornish produce with Asian influences, set in a picturesque harbor location.

Vegan and Vegetarian Options

Wild Café (Mawgan Porth): Offers a range of vegetarian and vegan dishes with a view of the sea.

The Bean Inn Vegetarian Café (St Ives): A cozy spot for vegetarian and vegan comfort food.

Potager Garden Café (Constantine): Set in a beautiful garden, offering plant-based dishes and homemade cakes.

Casual and Family-Friendly

Sam's On The Beach (Polkerris): Enjoy pizzas, burgers, and seafood in a relaxed beach setting.
Blas Burgerworks (St Ives): A great choice for families, offering a range of burgers, including vegetarian options.
Hub Box (Truro): Known for its American-style burgers and craft beers in a casual atmosphere.

Cafes and Bakeries

The Hidden Hut (Porthcurnick Beach): A beachside café known for its fresh salads, soups, and baked goods.
Da Bara Bakery Café (Indian Queens): Offers a range of freshly baked bread, pastries, and cakes.
Chapel Café (Port Isaac): A quaint café perfect for a light lunch or a cream tea.

REGION-SPECIFIC ITINERARIES FOR CORNWALL

Here are some tailored itineraries for different regions within Cornwall.

North Cornwall: Adventure and Surfing

Day 1: Newquay and Surrounding Beaches

- Morning: Surf lessons at Fistral Beach.
- Afternoon: Visit Newquay Zoo and relax at Towan Beach.
- Evening: Dine at one of the seafood restaurants in Newquay.

Day 2: Padstow and Coastal Wonders

- Morning: Explore the harbor town of Padstow; try a pasty from a local bakery.
- Afternoon: Cycle the Camel Trail to Wadebridge.
- Evening: Enjoy a meal at Rick Stein's Seafood Restaurant.

South Cornwall: Gardens and Maritime Heritage

Day 1: Falmouth and Maritime Museums

- Morning: Visit the National Maritime Museum Cornwall.
- Afternoon: Explore Pendennis Castle.
- Evening: Walk along Falmouth Harbour and dine in a waterside restaurant.

Day 2: Lost Gardens of Heligan and Charlestown

- Morning: Discover the Lost Gardens of Heligan.
- Afternoon: Stroll through the historic port of Charlestown.
- Evening: Enjoy dinner at a traditional Cornish inn.

West Cornwall: Art and History

Day 1: St Ives Artistic Exploration

- Morning: Visit the Tate St Ives and Barbara Hepworth Museum.
- Afternoon: Relax on Porthmeor Beach.
- Evening: Sample local cuisine in one of St Ives' eateries.

Day 2: Land's End and Minack Theatre

- Morning: Experience the rugged beauty of Land's End.
- Afternoon: Visit the Minack Theatre and Porthcurno Beach.
- Evening: Dinner in Penzance, exploring its historical streets.

The Lizard Peninsula: Nature and Tranquility

Day 1: Lizard Point and Kynance Cove

- Morning: Hike to Lizard Point, the southernmost tip of mainland Britain.
- Afternoon: Relax at Kynance Cove.
- Evening: Dinner at a local pub, enjoying fresh seafood.

Day 2: St Michael's Mount and Marazion

- Morning: Explore St Michael's Mount and its gardens.
- Afternoon: Enjoy the beaches and shops in Marazion.
- Evening: Sunset dinner with views of the Mount.

The Roseland Peninsula: Scenic Drives and Quiet Villages

Day 1: St Mawes and Roseland Coast

- Morning: Ferry trip to St Mawes and explore the castle.
- Afternoon: Drive through the picturesque villages of Roseland Peninsula.
- Evening: Seafood dinner in a coastal village.

Day 2: Truro and Trewithen Gardens

- Morning: Visit the Truro Cathedral and local markets.
- Afternoon: Stroll through the Trewithen Gardens.
- Evening: Enjoy a relaxed meal in one of Truro's restaurants.

FASCINATING FACT: CORNWALL'S COASTAL MARVELS

Cornwall is renowned for its breathtaking coastal landscapes, but there's a particularly fascinating aspect that truly sets it apart: it's incredibly varied and dynamic coastline. Here's why Cornwall's coastal marvels are a source of wonder:

Length and Diversity

Extensive Coastline: Stretching over 400 miles, Cornwall's coastline is one of the longest in the UK.

Varied Landscapes: From rugged cliffs and hidden coves to wide sandy beaches, the coastline offers a diverse array of landscapes within a relatively small area.

Geological Significance

Cornish Geology: Cornwall's geological history is incredibly rich, with rock formations dating back hundreds of millions of years. This geology has shaped its unique coastal features.

Mining Heritage: The coastline is dotted with remnants of Cornwall's mining past, particularly tin and copper mines, some of which are UNESCO World Heritage Sites.

Maritime History

Ancient Maritime Culture: Cornwall has a long-standing relationship with the sea, evident in its fishing harbors, maritime traditions, and folklore.

Shipwrecks and Exploration: The treacherous waters have been the site of numerous historical shipwrecks, adding an element of mystery and history to its shores.

Ecological Wonders

Marine Life: The Cornish coast is home to a rich variety of marine life, including seals, dolphins, and a multitude of seabirds.

Unique Flora: The climate and coastal conditions support unique plant life, some of which are found only in Cornwall.

Cultural and Artistic Inspiration

Artists' Haven: The natural beauty of Cornwall's coastline has inspired generations of artists, writers, and poets.

Cultural Celebrations: The coastal landscape plays a central role in many of Cornwall's festivals and cultural celebrations.

Recreational Paradise

Surfing and Water Sports: Cornwall is a haven for surfers and water sports enthusiasts, with beaches like Fistral and Polzeath renowned worldwide.

Coastal Walks: The South West Coast Path offers some of the most scenic walking routes in the UK, traversing the Cornish coastline.

PART 5: FOOD & DRINKS

South West England's culinary scene is as diverse and rich as its landscapes. Known for its bountiful coasts, lush farmlands, and traditional techniques, the region offers an array of unique flavors and dishes.

REGIONAL SPECIALTIES AND DELICACIES

1. Cornish Pasty

- **Description**: A traditional Cornish pasty is a hand-crafted pastry filled with beef, potatoes, swede (rutabaga), and onions. Originating from Cornwall's mining heritage, it was a practical, hearty meal for miners.

2. Cheddar Cheese

- **Origin**: From the village of Cheddar in Somerset, Cheddar cheese is celebrated for its rich, sometimes sharp flavor.

- **Varieties**: Ranging from mild to mature, it's renowned globally for its versatility and distinct taste.

3. Cream Tea

- **Components**: A quintessential British treat, it consists of scones, clotted cream, and strawberry jam.

- **Regional Debate**: Devon and Cornwall contest the correct order of applying cream and jam on scones.

4. Cider

- **Production**: Crafted from local apple varieties, cider is a staple beverage in the West Country.

- **Variety**: Ranging from sweet to dry, it's enjoyed in pubs and cider houses throughout the region.

5. Seafood

- **Coastal Bounty**: The region's extensive coastlines provide a rich variety of seafood like mussels, crabs, and fish.

- **Local Favorites**: Cornish mackerel and Devon crab are highly sought after for their freshness and flavor.

6. Dorset Blue Vinny

- **Characteristics**: A blue cheese known for its strong aroma and crumbly texture.

- **History**: Traditionally made in Dorset, it's a revival of a once nearly extinct cheese style.

7. Bath Buns

- **Description**: A sweet bun from Bath, often sprinkled with crushed sugar and topped with a candied cherry.

- **History**: Developed in the 18th century, it's a delightful tea-time treat.

8. Somerset Pork

- **Preparation**: Pork dishes in Somerset often incorporate cider and apples, reflecting the region's apple orchards.

- **Flavor Profile**: The combination yields a sweet and savory taste, unique to the region.

9. Gloucester Old Spot Pork

- **Breed**: A traditional English pig breed known for its high-quality meat.

- **Significance**: Revered for its marbling and flavor, it's a favorite in hearty West Country dishes.

10. Cornish Saffron Cake

- **Ingredients**: A rich, spiced cake made with saffron, currants, and raisins.

- **Occasions**: Often served during festivals and holidays, it's a Cornish celebration staple.

OTHER POPULAR FOOD ITEMS

Fisherman's Pie: A hearty seafood pie made with fish, shrimp, and creamy mashed potatoes.

Jugged Steak: A traditional Devon beef stew, slow-cooked with onions, carrots, and ale.

Ploughman's Lunch: A cold meal featuring local cheese (like Devon Blue), bread, pickles, and sometimes ham or other cold cuts.

Cider-Braised Pork: Slow-cooked pork in a rich cider sauce, often served with apples and root vegetables.

Somerset Pork Casserole: Pork cooked with apples, cider, and sage - reflecting the region's apple-growing heritage.

Bath Chap with Pease Pudding: A traditional dish of cured pork cheek served with pease pudding (a type of legume puree).

Welsh Rarebit: Although not exclusive to Somerset, it's a popular meal, featuring a savory cheese sauce over toasted bread.

Rabbit Pie: A game pie that's a part of traditional Somerset cuisine, often made with local herbs and cider.

Bath Chaps with Mustard Mash: A dish made from the lower jawbone of the pig, cured, boiled, and served with mustard-infused mashed potatoes.

Sally Lunn's Chicken and Bacon Pie: A savory pie using the famous Sally Lunn buns as a base or topping.

Beef and Ale Stew: A hearty stew often made with local Bath Ales.

Roast Dinner: Traditional Sunday roast, often with locally sourced meats and vegetables, served in many Bath restaurants.

Cornish Fish Stew: A robust stew made with locally caught fish, seafood, tomatoes, and herbs.

Cornish Game Hen: Roasted or grilled hens, often flavored with local herbs and served with seasonal vegetables.

Stargazy Pie Meal: This unique pie, made with pilchards or sardines, onions, and potatoes, can be a meal in itself.

PART 6: FAMILY-FRIENDLY ADVENTURES

Day 1: Fun in Cornwall

Morning:
Destination: Newquay Zoo (Trenance Gardens, Newquay)
Activities: Explore diverse animal exhibits and participate in interactive sessions.
Lunch: Enjoy a picnic in the nearby Trenance Gardens.

Afternoon:
Visit: Blue Reef Aquarium (Newquay)
Experience: Discover an underwater world with exciting marine life displays.
Highlight: Attend a feeding session or a guided tour.

Evening:
Dinner: Dine at a family-friendly restaurant in Newquay with a sea view.
Stay: Choose a family-oriented hotel or holiday park in Newquay.

Day 2: Discoveries in Devon

Morning:
Destination: Paignton Zoo (Totnes Rd, Paignton, Devon)
Adventure: Embark on a safari experience and learn about conservation efforts.
Breakfast: Grab a bite at the zoo's café offering kid-friendly options.

Afternoon:
Drive: Head to Dartmoor National Park.
Activity: Enjoy a family walk or pony trekking in the stunning moorlands.
Lunch: Have a picnic amidst Dartmoor's scenic backdrop.

Evening:
Explore: Visit the historic town of Totnes for its quaint charm.
Dinner: Try local Devonshire dishes in a traditional pub in Totnes.
Stay: Book a countryside cottage or farm stay for a rustic experience.

Morning: Explore the Roman Baths

Location: Abbey Churchyard, Bath, BA1 1LZ, UK

Activity: Discover the ancient Roman Baths with family-friendly audio guides.

Highlight: The Sacred Spring, Roman Temple, and Bath House.

Duration: Around 1.5 to 2 hours.

Tip: Check for family tickets for cost savings.

Mid-Morning: Bath City Farm

Location: Kelston View, Whiteway, Bath, BA2 1NW, UK

Activity: Interact with farm animals and enjoy the outdoor play area.

Duration: 1 to 1.5 hours.

Cost: Free entry, but donations are welcome.

Tip: Wear comfortable shoes and bring snacks for kids.

Lunch Break: Green Park Brasserie

Location: Green Park Station, Bath, BA1 1JB, UK

Offers: Kid-friendly menu and a relaxed atmosphere.

Special: Live music on certain days.

Afternoon: Victoria Park Playground

Location: Marlborough Ln, Bath, BA1 2NQ, UK

Features: A large playground with a variety of equipment for all ages.

Extra Fun: Miniature golf and a botanical garden nearby.

Duration: 2 to 3 hours.

Late Afternoon: Pulteney Bridge River Cruise

Location: Departs near Pulteney Bridge, Bath

Experience: Scenic boat trip along the River Avon.

Duration: 1 hour.

Evening: Dinner at The Real Italian Pizza Company

Location: 16 York St, Bath, BA1 1NG, UK

Family-Friendly: Offers a great selection of pizzas and pastas with a relaxed vibe.

Tip: Try their homemade gelato for dessert!

Optional Evening Activity: Bath Ghost Tour

For Older Kids: A fun and spooky walking tour exploring Bath's ghostly past.

Duration: Approximately 1 hour.

ADDITIONAL FAMILY ACTIVITIES

Interactive Museums in South West England

The Eden Project, Cornwall

Address: Bodelva, Cornwall, PL24 2SG, UK

Features:

- **Giant Biomes**: Houses the world's largest captive rainforest in one biome and a Mediterranean environment in another.
- **Interactive Exhibits**: Offers a range of hands-on experiences that engage children in learning about the environment, sustainability, and the natural world.
- **Educational Workshops**: Regularly hosts workshops and activities that are both fun and educational, tailored to different age groups.
- **Outdoor Gardens**: Extensive outdoor gardens that showcase a variety of plants and landscapes.
- **Seasonal Events**: Hosts special events like ice-skating in winter and music concerts in the summer, providing entertainment for all ages.
- **Family-Friendly Facilities**: Equipped with amenities like baby-changing facilities, picnic areas, and cafes with child-friendly menus.

Website: https://www.edenproject.com/

Estimated Cost: Ticket prices vary, with discounts for children, family tickets, and online booking. Generally, adult tickets are around £28.50, and child tickets are about £15 (prices subject to change).

Other Interactive Museums in the Region:

1. **We The Curious, Bristol**: A science and arts center with interactive exhibits and the UK's first 3D planetarium.
2. **The National Marine Aquarium, Plymouth**: The UK's largest public aquarium, offering educational experiences about marine life.
3. **Bristol Museum & Art Gallery**: Features a variety of exhibits, including ones dedicated to Egyptology and natural history, perfect for curious minds.
4. **The Roman Baths, Bath**: While not hands-on interactive, the museum offers a fascinating insight into Roman history with audio guides tailored for children.
5. **Dorset County Museum, Dorchester**: Offers family-friendly activities and exhibits on local history, including dinosaur fossils, appealing to young explorers.

Beach Fun: Spend a day at one of the many family-friendly beaches like Woolacombe Beach in Devon.

Adventure Parks: Visit Flambards Theme Park in Cornwall for rides and attractions suitable for all ages.

Nature Trails: Embark on family-friendly hikes like the Valley of Rocks walk in Lynton, Devon.

Travel Tips for Families

Recommended Child-Friendly Eateries:

1. **Jamie Oliver's Fifteen, Cornwall**: Not only does it offer a stunning view of the beach, but it also provides crayons and coloring sheets to keep little ones busy.

2. **The Rockpool, Gwithian**: Beachside café perfect for families after a day of surfing or playing in the sand. Offers a great children's menu and outdoor play area.

3. **River Cottage Canteen, Devon**: Known for its organic and locally sourced menu, it offers a delightful kids' menu and a welcoming atmosphere for families.

4. **The Cornish Arms, Tavistock, Devon**: A traditional pub with a family-friendly setting. Offers a special menu for kids and outdoor space for play.

5. **The Donkey Sanctuary, Sidmouth**: Not just a sanctuary for donkeys but also hosts a café with ample space for kids and a variety of kid-friendly food options.

6. **The Big Sheep, Bideford, Devon**: An amusement park with its own restaurant that caters to families, providing both fun activities and kid-friendly meals.

Printed in Great Britain
by Amazon

42284358R00066